"Wise and eminently practical, We [...]
book. Elsdon's transformational st[...]
sights provide wonderful ways to reimagine mission and ministry in diverse
contexts. Take, read, and put into practice!"

— **L. Gregory Jones**
president of Belmont University

"*We Aren't Broke* does an excellent job of digging into challenging topics and
highlighting new ways for the church to utilize its assets and reclaim its position as the transformational agent of change in our communities."

— **Derrick Morgan**
retired NFL linebacker and managing partner at KNGDM Group

"Mark Elsdon has written a book on money in the church that is both smart
and wise. The smart part of his book is that he opens up important specific
resources for good money management and investment. The wise part of
his book is that he appeals to faith in order to imagine afresh the uses of our
resources. Elsdon's own life experience provides an elemental case study
for his exposition."

— **Walter Brueggemann**
Columbia Theological Seminary

"An insightful, first-person tour through the challenges of funding church-
based ministries and exploring our relations of faith and finance. By combin-
ing reflections on his own journey with discussions of the best thinking and
practices of innovative finance, Elsdon offers a solid vision of how money
and mission may be integrated to advance the critical work of the church in
the current century."

— **Jed Emerson**
author of *The Purpose of Capital*

"*We Aren't Broke* is a welcome resource that so many churches need now,
and Mark Elsdon is just the right guide. With wisdom and expertise gained
through years of working alongside religious organizations as well as entrepreneurs, investors, and community advocates, Elsdon provides the perfect mix of
practical advice with hope, creativity, and theological imagination."

— **David P. King**
director of the Lake Institute on Faith and Giving at Indiana University

"Mark Elsdon asks us, 'If the purpose of capital is to make good in the world with what God has lent us, and the way we go about growing that capital makes a difference, how then are we to think about the role capital plays in perpetuating or eliminating injustice in the world?' This is a critical question for consideration, one of many that Elsdon so thoughtfully reflects upon in this important book."

— **Morgan Simon**
author of *Real Impact: The New Economics of Social Change*

"Drawing deeply from the worlds of business, mission-driven organizational leadership, and personal experiences of transformational college ministry, this book is part leadership workbook and part theological/ethical reflection on the value of investing in doing good—a must-read for pastors, social entrepreneurs, and people of faith who want to change the world."

— **Frank M. Yamada**
executive director of the Association of Theological Schools

"I've read the parable of the rich young fool from Luke 12 over a thousand times and never noticed how conventional wisdom about money is the very thing that Scripture tells us is foolish! I'm thankful for Mark Elsdon's theological, economic, and practical road map that shows us how to be wise according to the Kingdom of God's standard."

— **David M. Bailey**
founder and CEO of Arrabon

"Mark Elsdon masterfully shares his experience of making faith-focused impact investments from the early stages through the long term. He reminds us that there is great power in the current economic state of religious institutions—the question is, what impact will they seek? You will finish this book feeling motivated and guided on how church assets can be directed to seek positive impact."

— **Kate Walsh**
Global Impact Investing Network

# WE AREN'T BROKE

*Uncovering Hidden Resources for Mission and Ministry*

Mark Elsdon

WILLIAM B. EERDMANS PUBLISHING COMPANY

GRAND RAPIDS, MICHIGAN

The author, Mark Elsdon, does not offer specific investment recommendations or advice to the reader of this material, which is general in nature and should not be considered a comprehensive review or analysis of the topics discussed. This material is intended to be impersonal in nature and does not take into account the individual circumstances of readers or any institutions they may represent. The author is not an attorney or accountant and does not provide legal, tax, or accounting advice.

A reader should not make personal financial or investment decisions based solely upon reading this material. This material is not a substitute for, or the same as, a consultation with an investment advisor. Investment strategies have the potential for loss, and investment advisors cannot offer any guarantees or promises of success. Despite efforts to be accurate and current, this material may contain out-of-date information; the author will not be under an obligation to advise the reader of any subsequent changes related to the topics discussed in this material.

Wm. B. Eerdmans Publishing Co.
4035 Park East Court SE, Grand Rapids, Michigan 49546
www.eerdmans.com

27 26 25 24 23 22    2 3 4 5 6 7

ISBN 978-0-8028-7898-4

**Library of Congress Cataloging-in-Publication Data**

Names: Elsdon, Mark, 1977– author.
Title: We aren't broke : uncovering hidden resources for mission and ministry / Mark Elsdon.
Description: Grand Rapids, Michigan : William B. Eerdmans Publishing Company, [2021] | Includes bibliographical references and index. | Summary: "A guide for churches and missional organizations in using hidden assets, such as property and investments, to transform communities and thrive in the face of financial difficulty"—Provided by publisher.
Identifiers: LCCN 2020051824 | ISBN 9780802878984
Subjects: LCSH: Missions. | Finance—Religious aspects—Christianity.
Classification: LCC BV2063 .E455 2021 | DDC 266—dc23
LC record available at https://lccn.loc.gov/2020051824

*For Emma and Sophie,*
*who are the reason we must do things differently*
*and who will show us how*

# Contents

**PART TWO**

*Ingredients to Make It Work*

# Contents

# Foreword

The good news here is in the title: *We Aren't Broke.* The church is not broke financially. Nor is it broke spiritually or missionally. It is, however, ripe for renewal—in many ways and on many levels. And this fine book provides superb guidance toward these ends. It is a book of wisdom born of experience. And the experience and insight Mark Elsdon provides here will be of great value to all who read and learn from the gifts it has to offer.

Right out of seminary, Mark Elsdon and his spouse, Erica Liu, got started in ministry as copastors at Pres House, the Presbyterian campus ministry at the University of Wisconsin. At the time, the ministry there was on its last legs. The building in which it was housed, once a large, beautiful one, had fallen into serious disrepair. So had the ministry's finances. And worst of all, the students had abandoned it.

Even so, the campus ministry's board of directors was eager to give it one more try. Fortunately, the board called Mark and Erica, who had just recently graduated from Princeton Seminary, to be their new campus ministers. Aware of all the difficulties, they nonetheless decided to accept the invitation and give it a shot. It took time and patience, but step by step and with a lot of thought and experimentation, they and the Board together found ways to cultivate a whole new communal reality and spirit at Pres House that has also infected the larger UW campus.

Over the years, Mark and Erica's experience at Pres House (where they still serve) has given rise to a still larger vision—the one described at length here in *We Aren't Broke.* This larger effort Mark is engaged in is helping us all find ways of "reimagining mission and money for innovation and transformation." All five of those key words—"reimagining," "mission," "money," "innovation," and "transformation"—are essential. And they all have to be put into play in ways that complement and enhance one other.

*We Aren't Broke* is a guidebook of the very best kind. Each chapter provides both penetrating insight and practical guidance regarding the issues and moves that every institution or organization needs in order to address and to serve its constituency, thrive institutionally, and, above all, fulfill its mission. This includes, of course, its ability to accumulate adequately and deploy wisely the resources needed to do so. Indeed, Elsdon's discussions of these issues permeate the book and provide an extraordinary compendium of financial strategies that individuals and institutions can employ.

Finally, *We Aren't Broke* is richly ethical and theological. Elsdon's aim is to cultivate, guide, and encourage "redemptive entrepreneurs and social enterprises." And that sensibility pervades this book in a way that is both welcoming and substantive. His chapter "Creating a New Future by Repairing the Past" is a powerful chapter on the uses and misuses of money—and of persons (including slavery)— throughout our history.

In sum, the stories Elsdon has to tell throughout this book and the wise counsel he has to offer are very much worth reading, both individually and in groups. So I hope and expect that *We Aren't Broke* gets a very wide reading. It is the best and most accessible book I know of for helping individuals as well as a wide variety of religious, educational, civic, and service institutions and their leaders to think creatively and practice wisely the kinds of institutional and collaborative efforts that "reimagine mission" and raise and deploy the resources we need for the sake of innovation and transformation in our society and culture.

— *Craig Dykstra*

# Preface

"We can pinpoint the date when our denomination will cease to exist. People just aren't coming to church on Sunday morning anymore."

"How do we get young people to come to church?!?"

"The legacy of racial and economic injustice in our community is overwhelming. And our denomination has been a part of the problem in the past. What can we do about it now?"

"I'm not sure we will be open in ten years. There just isn't enough money to keep going."

"Look at all the needs in our community! We can barely keep our lights on. How are we supposed to meet those pressing needs?"

"We are closing five churches in our town. What are we going to do with the empty buildings?"

These are all questions and worries I've heard raised over meals, in denominational meetings, at conferences, and on video conference calls in the past couple of years. You may have heard some of them yourself. You may have spoken some of them yourself. I know I have.

These are all very real concerns. Many Christian churches and related institutions in the United States are facing an imminent crisis, or are at least struggling. Attendance is down. Funding is harder to come by. Churches are closing, and buildings are being sold. Climate change, wealth inequality, and racial tension are massive problems facing our communities that the church is struggling to respond to.

People are no longer drawn to traditional church services and programming in the ways they once were. We often feel broke and powerless to do much about it all. We continually try to do more with less. Fewer people. Fewer dollars. Fewer churches.

Just as I was finishing this book, the world was rocked by COVID-19, a virulent coronavirus that forced us to stay more than six feet away from anyone we didn't live with, brought the economy to a standstill, and moved most church activity online. At the time of this writing, it remains unclear how long these restrictions will be in place and what the long-term impact will be on society and the church. But we can be sure that we will not emerge from this pandemic unchanged. The crisis of mission and money we are facing in the church has suddenly been amplified and accelerated by the virus and its social and economic implications. The questions of how we serve our community and how we fund our mission are more urgent and pressing than ever.

But there is hope.

This is a book about abundance, possibility, and hope; about what we have rather than what we don't have. It is a book about how the wealth of creativity, perseverance, and resources that exists in church institutions can be put to work for mission in new ways. It invites us to think differently about the property and money God has entrusted to us. This is a book that I hope will spark new ways of thinking and being in the world so that together we can transform communities, address injustice and inequality, and sustain effective ministry during a time of major change.

Because we aren't broke. We have much, and there is much to do.

# Introduction: We Aren't Broke

It was the second time he had relapsed in just a matter of months and one of countless times he had turned to heroin in the past few years. He had tried to quit for good. And tried. And tried. But the pull of a drug that takes the lives of more than fifteen thousand Americans each year was too much. It didn't matter that he had almost died of an overdose in the past. It didn't matter that his life had been derailed and he had hurt most of the people who loved him most. It didn't matter that he had gone through two inpatient treatment programs and had already relapsed once in the sober housing program he was now enrolled in. It didn't even matter that he was back in school as a student at the University of Wisconsin–Madison for the second time with a chance to finish and graduate this time. The draw of the drug was too strong. The disease was too powerful. What more could he do? Was there any hope of escape? And what, if anything, could the church do to help?

A lot, it turns out. The church could do a lot.

Peter (whose name has been changed for this story) was living in the Pres House Apartments as part of a sober housing program called Next Step when this latest relapse happened. He had relapsed once in the program already. But this time, rather than write him off as a lost cause, the staff and other residents held him accountable to the recovery plan he had put in place for himself and supported him through this latest setback. This time it worked. With the help of his

Next Step roommates and other resources, Peter moved deeper into his journey of recovery. He began to find success in school and make meaningful friendships on campus. He started emerging from the darkness into light. Hope was reborn.

By the time Peter had graduated from college with a 3.5 grade point average and a degree in computer engineering and taken a job at a well-known firm, he had run a marathon and mended relationships with many of those he had hurt while using heroin. He was a peer mentor in the Next Step program and an officer in the campus recovery student organization. And most importantly, he was sober. Peter's life had been transformed by living in an apartment building that was built by a Presbyterian campus ministry, on church-owned land, financed with an impact investment from a denominational endowment.

And he is not the only one. Eighty percent of the participants in the Next Step sober housing program at Pres House Apartments over the years have either graduated from degree programs or remained sober or both. At a time when the opioid crisis is wreaking havoc on communities all over the country, this program has saved lives, and has saved Wisconsinites almost half a million dollars in costs associated with addiction. At a time when the church is struggling to figure out what role it is playing in our world—where fewer people attend worship services but more "wicked problems" need our attention— the church was there for Peter and his friends.[1]

What may be most remarkable of all is that the building that changed Peter's life was built on a parking lot owned by Presbyterian campus ministry. I know, because I parked in that lot on my first day as a pastor.

\* \* \*

1. The term "wicked problem" was first used by design theorist Horst Rittel and has come to refer to social problems that are extremely difficult or impossible to solve due to the complexity of issues involved. The term in this context does not mean "evil."

I first learned about Pres House through a phone call during my senior year of seminary. A pastor from the presbytery where my spouse, Erica, and I were candidates for ordination invited us to consider an opening for campus copastors at this place called Pres House in Madison, Wisconsin. He had been working with the board of directors as a consultant to help them update their strategic plan for the future. The plan was simple and ambitious: hire pastors, start a new campus ministry, and develop the property for long-term sustainability and ministry.

I don't remember much about that initial conversation, because our lives were a blur at that point. We had just had our first child, and she was only a few days old. As Erica recalls, we really should not have been asked to make any reasonable decisions at that moment. But about a month after that first phone call with members of the search committee at Pres House, we found ourselves driving past the spectacular sight of the Wisconsin state capitol into Madison for the first time in our lives. And a few months later we changed our permanent address to Madison, WI.

Looking back on it all, I am not sure what prompted us to come to Pres House for our first pastoral call. There were zero students involved in the campus ministry. Zero. Despite a rich legacy of ministry going back to 1907, Pres House was dormant when we arrived. Students at the University of Wisconsin don't attend church in significant numbers, and they certainly weren't showing up at Pres House. The historic church building was in dire need of updating—the roof was leaking, and I quickly found myself fixing the toilet with paper clips, just to keep it running. There wasn't enough money in the annual budget to fund our salaries. Pres House seemed pretty broke.

I guess we must have seen some potential. Or we were just naive and foolish. Maybe a little of both.

So, my first week on the job, I was sprawled on the floor of my office putting together a desk from a kit bought from Office Depot. I think it was day two of screwing the thousands of little screws into the particle-board desk when a freshman wandered into the building.

He stuck his head into the chaos of my office and asked me, "Hey, does 'Pres' stand for Presbyterian?"

"Yes!" I replied. "It does!"

"Cool," he replied. "What happens here? I grew up Presbyterian and just moved to campus. What can I join?"

After a brief pause, I decided to go for honesty; after all, it was my first official week as a pastor. "Nothing!" I replied. "Nothing is happening here at all . . . but we'd love for you to join us in helping to start something new."

And so the rebirth began. Over the next year, after much prayer, discussion, and study, we had gathered a small group of students to form the core of a new community at Pres House.[2] A small spark of hope was kindled in the embers of a remarkable legacy of ministry.

But even as we began gathering a new community of students, we were asking ourselves how this spark would grow into the sustaining warmth of a real fire without fuel. We were spending down our endowment funds at an unsustainable pace. Our building was literally falling apart around us. Long-time, faithful donors gave just ten thousand dollars per year, and even less came from the denomination. This was hardly enough to sustain a historic property, pastors, staff, and the full-fledged campus ministry we and our board of directors dreamed of. Before we even began rebuilding, we knew that without some new approach to the financial model, it was only a matter of time before we would run out of money and have to close up for good. There was a spark of hope—but where would the fuel come from to keep the flame alive?

We started with the property and an eighty-year-old dream. Our board of directors had updated a long-held vision to build student

2. I will refer to "we" and "us" a lot throughout this book. This is for two reasons. I serve at Pres House as copastor with my spouse, Erica Liu. All our work has been a team effort, and I could never have been successful at this work without her equal partnership. In a similar manner, the rebirth of Pres House involved a lot of committed and gifted people—our board of directors, student leaders, donors, staff, and many others. Nothing successful happens in a vacuum or by a lone leader. All these efforts are collective. We did this work together.

housing on the parking lot next to the historic Pres House chapel. At the same time that we began to relaunch student ministry, we started planning for the construction of a seven-story apartment building. Meetings with the architects took place around our kitchen table while our baby daughter slept in the other room. The board was willing to take a huge risk and dream big, so we borrowed $17 million for construction of the new facility and complete renovation of the historic chapel building. After two years of planning and one year of construction, we opened the Pres House Apartments for 250 residents three years after we first arrived in Madison.

That is the much-condensed version of how my parking space was turned into the living community that changed the trajectory of Peter's life and helped free him from the tyranny of heroin.

Sixteen years later, we now serve more than eight hundred students and young adults each year at Pres House through Sunday worship, large campus events, small groups, service and justice activities, and intentional communities in the Pres House Apartments. One example is the Next Step program for residents in addiction recovery that helps heroin addicts stay in school and rebuild their lives. Other communities are themed around vocational discernment, wellness, volunteer service, Christian practices, and so on. Demand is so high for our intentional-living programs that we are raising more money to fund more scholarships, and there are wait lists every year. We recently launched Candid, a wellness program aimed at helping students address the pressing issues of resilience and mental health by supporting them in the context of community. Some of our activities at Pres House, like a weekly worship service on Sunday afternoons, are explicitly Christian in content. Others are designed to be accessible and meaningful for students of all religious backgrounds. All of what we do is grounded in the love and grace of Jesus Christ for every person, even if we don't require or expect those we serve to share that same faith commitment.

We have measured the impact of our mission and have discovered some powerful outcomes. Residents in the Pres House Apartments typically triple the number of people they know in our building from fall to spring—a vastly different outcome from standard student apartment buildings. In a typical year, 100 percent of surveyed campus church participants say they feel cared for by the Pres House community and would recommend Pres House to a friend. On a campus where only 10 percent of the student body is nonwhite, between 25 and 45 percent of attendees on any given Sunday are students of color. More than 90 percent of participants experience opportunities to interact with people different from them, and the vast majority report learning or trying something new in their spiritual life each year through our programs.

Even while working with a population famous for not being interested in church, Pres House has been able to engage thousands of students in just the past few years alone. We have found new ways to meet the real needs of students. The little corner of the church located on Library Mall at the university is deeply involved in addressing the "wicked problems" of our community, from the opioid crisis, to student mental health, to racial tension on campus. I am a pastor who loves to preach, but our Sunday worship service is not the only, nor perhaps even the primary, place that students experience the grace of Jesus Christ, are challenged to grow in their sense of purpose, and are sent out into the world around them to serve and lead. That is now happening in their living rooms, throughout all aspects of their lives, and virtually 24/7. Instead of engaging for only one hour per week on Sunday, residents of the Pres House Apartments are involved in their very homes for more than a hundred hours per week.

The social enterprise at Pres House has had a transformative effect on our finances as well. Our budget has grown 1,500 percent, from about $150,000 annually in 2004 to about $2.4 million today. Since we gained a solid financial footing, traditional fund-raising has taken off, with more than $5.5 million raised from individuals, churches, and foundations. Because our overhead is covered by program revenue, 100 percent of each donated dollar directly supports students.

We found the fuel needed to grow the spark into a real flame. And we found that fuel literally in our backyard. In our parking lot. We built a financially successful and influential social enterprise on church-owned property. And in doing so, we totally transformed a historic institution and the lives of thousands upon thousands of young adults now and into the future.

\* \* \*

When I first pulled into my parking spot at Pres House as a brand-new minster, the church was facing two major problems that, while not necessarily universal, are widely shared by much of the Christian church in the United States. These two core problems lie beneath the anxieties mentioned in the preface to this book.

1.  Individuals and communities are longing for different expressions of lived faith that move beyond the traditional programs of churches. Traditional church programs are often no longer engaging people nor helping people engage the world. We are facing serious crises such as climate change, racial injustice, opioid addiction, income inequality, and more. How are we going to tackle these "wicked problems" with innovative solutions through new expressions of the church in the world?

2.  Churches and church-related institutions (seminaries, colleges, etc.) are struggling with an economic model that is increasingly coming up short in funding mission, especially the kind of mission that addresses the wicked problems we want to solve. The way we have funded mission and ministry in the past is no longer working. How will we generate sustainable forms of revenue to support mission?[3]

I have been fortunate enough to participate in a ministry approach that has addressed both of these problems. Providing a purposeful

3. When I use the term "mission" in this book, I do not mean it in a necessarily Christian or religious sense. I use it in the sense that any effective organization that wants to accomplish something, including a business, must have a clear and compelling mission that drives its activity and focuses direction.

and supportive living environment at Pres House has allowed us to engage and serve students like Peter and thousands more in the issues that really matter to them. While Sunday worship is central to our mission, we have gone much deeper and wider with our ministry, transforming areas of students' lives that previously we were absent from. And we have found a sustainable way to pay for this work. While donor funds are still essential to accomplishing our mission, our earned income has completely changed the financial calculus and funded our growth. Most powerfully of all, the mission outcomes and financial outcomes are intimately and fully integrated. Success in mission leads to success financially, and the reverse is also true. We have reconnected money to mission and mission to money.

My story at Pres House is one particular example. It is not necessarily a model in and of itself. And nothing short of God's own hand will solve these deep problems in all contexts. But there is real potential to put the dynamic power of *redemptive entrepreneurship*[4] to work alongside the sustaining fuel of *church-owned capital assets* (i.e., property and investment) for lasting innovation and transformation in our churches and communities. And these tools are available to us right now, in the church today. This book is an invitation to innovate and transform lives and institutions using the abundance of gifts that God has given us. There is enormous possibility and hope. We are most certainly not broke.

* * *

4. The term "redemptive entrepreneurship" was used at a gathering of faith-based entrepreneurs, funders, and thought leaders at the UnFamous 2019 conference in Seattle to try to describe this emerging movement. The term is also used by Praxis Labs, an incubator for faith-based social entrepreneurs. Other terms are often used in a related manner, such as "faith-based social enterprise," "social business," "social entrepreneurship," etc. There are limits and questions in the use of all these terms. I will typically use the terms "social enterprise" and "redemptive entrepreneurship" throughout this book.

Books have to be printed in a linear fashion with one chapter coming after another and one idea following from another. But this subject doesn't fit neatly into that format. The ideas here are not linear but are more akin to a multifaced shape looked at from different angles. Rather than building an argument step-by-step for how we have resources for mission and capital to fund our ministry differently, I will look at this central thesis from different theological and practical angles.

In part 1 of the book, I invite us to reimagine the way we go about mission and our relationship with money in the church. In chapter 1 I continue the story of Pres House and describe how financial necessity and desperation led us to design a resource model using church-owned investment assets as capital for financing the Pres House Apartments, which produced a triple-bottom-line return: mission impact, financial sustainability for Pres House, and financial return for our denominational investor, which in turn furthered its mission impact. This chapter also introduces the concept of impact investing that I later learned is a well-developed and rapidly growing field.

Chapter 2 looks at the financial model we have employed in the church in recent history. This can be summarized as a "two-pocket" model, where money is raised or earned from investment in one pocket and then spent on mission out of the other pocket. This chapter begins the exploration of what happens to our money when it is invested traditionally.

Chapter 3 asks the question, "What is the highest and best use of our capital?" I unpack the parable of the rich fool who builds bigger barns in order to save up for a future day that never comes, rather than releasing what God has given him into the world.

Chapter 4 encourages us to apply two important principles from the story of the rich fool to our use of capital in the church: (1) all that we have is a loan from God; and (2) we need to control money rather than let it control us. We have an opportunity to open the barn doors rather than build bigger barns—in other words, to put our capital to work in the world.

Chapter 5 pivots and takes a look at the impact of our invested money from a different angle. All investment has impact, for good or for ill. We have explored other aspects of the life cycle of money (earning, giving, spending) in the church but have in some ways neglected deeper conversations about the saving part of the life cycle. Where our money sleeps at night matters, and this chapter explores that.

Chapter 6 dives more deeply into questions about injustice and how many of us and our institutions have profited from systemic racism and inequality. This chapter suggests that putting capital to work differently has potential to address these injustices and create a new future by repairing the past.

After a number of chapters exploring how we relate to money, especially investment, chapter 7 returns to opportunities for hope—that redemptive entrepreneurship and impact investing have potential to lead to transformative impact in our communities and sustainable funding to carry out that work.

Invested assets are one form of capital that the church can release differently for transformation and innovation. But another form of capital is even more widespread and often underutilized: property. Churches own vast amounts of property in almost every community in the nation. Chapter 8 explores how the use of church-owned property can be reimagined and repurposed at a time when many congregations are closing and important questions are being asked about the use of church buildings and land.

Chapter 9 closes out part 1 of the book by looking at some of the barriers and perils of engaging in social enterprise and impact investing in the church. There are risks associated with this work, and there are barriers to effective implementation and application. We would do well to engage with eyes wide open.

In part 2 of the book (chapters 10 through 12), I turn attention to five ingredients that make redemptive entrepreneurship and impact investing work well from the perspective of the entrepreneur on the one hand and the investor on the other. These ingredients seek to address the barriers and perils noted in chapter 9 and help keep us focused on using the tools of social enterprise and impact investment for aims consistent with the gospel. These ingredients are derived from years of on-the-ground experience as well as from integrating theological reflection and business acumen into practical approaches that really make a difference.

I conclude the book by raising questions and offering suggestions for where we might go from here. I end with an invitation for each of us to consider how the capital resources we are connected with personally, and through our organizations, can be put to work for even more good in the world.

Finally, a comment about terminology and audience. This book is designed to be read by individuals and teams with a wide range of familiarity with business and investing language. If you happen to be seminary-trained, and attended a traditional seminary as I did, you may not have learned much, if anything, about these terms and concepts. That is okay. I have attempted to explain the concepts in ways that apply to readers who are familiar with investment and business. For those that are not, I have included a tailored glossary at the end. You will find common investment terms listed in the glossary, but instead of being defined as in a business textbook or on Wikipedia, these terms are defined in a way that is specifically relevant to redemptive entrepreneurship and faith-based work.

Now, let's dive in, for there are lots of resources and much to do. As we reimagine our mission and money, we will find that we are not broke. Possibility and hope abound.

# PART ONE

# Reimagining Mission and Money for Innovation and Transformation

The church has been doing "mission and money" since its inception in the book of Acts. Amid its many successes have come, if not failure, at least staleness. In this part of the book we will revisit some of the church's historic approaches to money and reimagine a more fruitful and life-giving way to align money and mission.

Taking our cues from the example of Pres House Apartments in Madison, Wisconsin, we start by learning one way to design a resource model using church-owned investment assets to further the ministry of the church.

Many churches and related institutions own enormous amounts of property and huge sums of investment assets, both of which can be used differently for mission. These assets are hidden in plain sight. Two concepts we explore in depth, redemptive entrepreneurship and impact investing, have the potential to lead to transformative impact in our communities and provide sustainable funding to carry out that work.

The church isn't broke by any means. God has lent us manifold financial gifts. Reimagining how we handle them—rather than allowing them to handle us—is the subject of this first part of the book.

# 1

## Uncovering Abundance

W e can't do anything with what we don't have, ... but we do have something," Pastor Michael Mather said to me and a group of Christian leaders gathered at his church in Indianapolis. Mike had just spent a couple of hours sharing the story of church and community transformation at Broadway United Methodist Church. The key to transformation at Mather's church was simple yet profound: identifying and celebrating the many "somethings" that people in the community had and encouraging them to put those gifts to use.[1]

Listening to Michael, I realized this had happened at Pres House in our rebirth. Where some saw only scarcity in a dormant campus ministry—a crumbling building and a basic parking lot—others saw possibility . . . *something*. But before I get to that, allow me to fill in a little more of the history of how we at Pres House ended up feeling broke.

Pres House was founded in 1907 to serve students at the growing public land-grant college that has become the University of Wisconsin–Madison. Like many campus ministries at the beginning of the twentieth century, this new student community flourished. By the early 1920s, it had outgrown its space and needed a new build-

---

1. Michael Mather has written a book about this titled *Having Nothing, Possessing Everything: Finding Abundant Communities in Unexpected Places* (Grand Rapids: Eerdmans, 2018).

ing, so land was purchased right on the main quad of campus and a beautiful neo-Gothic church was built.[2] Plans to build dorms for students had also been drawn up, but those dreams came crashing down with the stock market and the Great Depression. But the ministry continued to grow, and by the 1950s Pres House, as it had become known, was thriving. The congregation of many hundreds was entirely student run. The only nonstudents in leadership were the pastors, the office manager, and the choir director. All the elders and deacons were twenty-something college students, and they ran a full-fledged church.

Then the years of decline began. Membership numbers plummeted as the 1960s progressed and church became suspect rather than the place to be each Sunday. Its unique quality as a student-run church proved to be its rapid undoing when students stopped attending church in significant numbers. This story of decline was not unique to Pres House, for it was also happening with other campus churches at the University of Wisconsin and around the country. In the time it takes for a freshman to become a senior and graduate, this entirely student-run church had disappeared. The official congregation was dissolved in 1969.

The ministry evolved and took different forms in the following decades. There were some good years for funding and ministry and some not-so-good years. By the late 1990s, the Synod of Lakes and Prairies of the Presbyterian Church, the parent body of Pres House, decided to sell the property because it was costly to maintain and no long-term viable ministry plan was visible. Fortunately, the attempted sale was scuttled by alumni and local leaders in Madison, who pointed out how shortsighted it was to sell property in the very center of a

2. It is important to acknowledge that Pres House, and the University of Wisconsin, is located on the traditional, ancestral homelands of the Ho-Chunk people, whose land was stolen from them in 1832.

major state university. The synod did sell properties at the University of Minnesota and the University of Iowa with the intent of putting the proceeds into a fund to support campus ministry. Those properties are now gone. Much of the money from those sales has been used up. And Presbyterian campus ministry on those campuses has struggled to gain traction. The contrast between what happened where property was sold and what happened at Pres House could not be any starker.

Where some saw an aging building with a leaky roof, the inspired folks who resisted the sale of Pres House saw a beautiful building that had been a spiritual and physical home to tens of thousands of college students for more than ninety years. Where some saw an underutilized parking lot behind the old chapel that could easily be sold, others saw property located in the very heart of a world-class university that could become something much more than a patch of asphalt and parking meters. Where some saw a struggling program and uncertainty about how to serve students, others saw a legacy of God's spirit at work in and through Pres House that was ripe for resurrection.

When Erica and I stood on the main quad of the University of Wisconsin and looked up at the empty, somewhat dilapidated building, wondering if we should move across the country to a state we had never even visited, we said to ourselves, "Well, . . . they have something."

I have found that often in the church we get stuck on the first half of Mather's phrase: we can't do anything with what we don't have. "We don't have enough people. We don't have enough energy. We don't have enough money." That last one especially—we don't have enough money. I get it. I am a realist (sometimes even a pessimist). We don't have as much of some of those things as we once did in some areas of the church. But we do have something. Lots of somethings actually. And "imagining abundance," to borrow the title of Kerry Alys Robinson's book, is a far more exciting, effective, truthful, and dare

I say, faithful approach to take.[3] We do have something. I wanted to approach my ministry with that way of thinking.

I didn't realize how quickly this way of thinking was going to be tested in my work at Pres House. The story of rebirth told in the introduction to this book sounds wonderful. And the good parts are all true. But there were many difficult and trying times along the way. We almost lost it all when the city of Madison slapped us with a huge property tax bill we were not expecting. In order to survive we had to work with state government to pass a revised law clarifying property tax exemption for property like ours. We had trouble filling the apartment building in the early years and went through three property management companies before we found one that treated students with respect and effectively leased the rooms. We ran out of money during construction to repair the leaking roof and were saved at the last minute by what can only be described as a miraculous quarter-million-dollar donation. At one point I wasn't sure where payroll was going to come from for our incredibly hardworking staff (and myself).

And then came one of the biggest challenges of all: the financial crisis of 2008. Within one year of opening our building, a financial crisis erupted that left virtually no person or institution in the United States and across much of the world untouched, including Pres House. We had borrowed most of the $17 million it cost to build the Pres House Apartments and carry out a complete renovation of the historic chapel building. Shortly after 2008 we were due to refinance that debt. And like many unfortunate homeowners at that time, we found ourselves underwater. Not because we couldn't pay our bills. Not because we had borrowed too much. But because lending regulations had changed and the bank-assessed value of our property had dropped. We were short $2.5 million. What were we going to do with

---

3. Kerry Alys Robinson, *Imagining Abundance: Fundraising, Philanthropy, and a Spiritual Call to Service* (Collegeville, MN: Liturgical Press, 2014).

what we didn't have? Just as things seemed to be on the upswing, yet again we faced a crisis of scarcity.

Still, even in the most dire of circumstances, we had something. We just needed to look a bit beyond our immediate circumstances and think a little more creatively about what resources were available.

## Investing in Mission Impact

As the executive director of a faith-based nonprofit, I have done a lot of fund-raising over the years, and I often hear folks say there just aren't the resources in the church that there were back in the glory days. And it is true that some forms of funding have declined; funding for campus ministry is almost entirely extinct in most parts of the country; and declining membership has led to less money for many churches and other institutions.

But in the mainline church ecosystem, and in many parts of the wider big C "Church," we have a lot of assets. A lot of capital. Incredibly valuable property in A-plus locations. Buildings. And massive endowments. We are not broke. In fact, the member organizations of the Interfaith Center on Corporate Responsibility (ICCR) have more than $400 billion of invested assets under management (that is billion, with a *b*). It is simply not true that there is no money in the church. It is just that most of it is invested in corporations like Facebook and Amazon. So I wondered, what would it look like if some of that money were invested in a faith-based social enterprise at Pres House?

It turned out that the Synod of Lakes and Prairies of the PCUSA had about $10 million in an endowment invested in stocks, bonds, and other market instruments. They invested that money fairly traditionally and used the income from those investments to fund their programming. But what if they invested some of it directly in one of their own ministries?

After a year of extensive conversations and negotiations, the synod decided to diversify their investments by moving one-quarter of that endowment into real estate. They invested $2.5 million in real estate at the University of Wisconsin–Madison, real estate owned and operated for the purpose of serving students through Pres House. The very same synod that a decade earlier was focused on what we didn't have and almost sold Pres House, now saw very clearly and powerfully what the church did have—capital for mission and ministry. With their catalytic impact investment, we were able to secure favorable financing terms on the rest of our debt. Since then the synod has provided us with stable capital, while we provide them with a return on their investment that they in turn use for their programming. And thousands of students at the University of Wisconsin have been served by the church. As Jeremey Balkin says, "Finance is about matching ideas with capital, and capital with great ideas."[4] That is what we did. It has been a win-win-win. Their impact investment produces a triple-bottom-line return.

Three tools had come together. We launched a meaningful and financially successful *social enterprise*[5] using *church-owned property* in a prime location and financed in part by impact investment using *church-owned investment assets*.

A few years after we closed on this deal, I asked the synod treasurer, who had been the driving force behind the move, what had led the synod to do something creative and somewhat risky (not typical

---

4. Jeremy Balkin, *Investing with Impact: Why Finance Is a Force for Good* (New York: Bibliomotion, 2015), 59.

5. "Social enterprise" has a number of definitions, but when I use it here I am talking about any form of mission-based activity doing good in the world that also generates revenue from sales or earned income (as distinct from donated money). Social enterprises can take many different legal forms and can be either nonprofit or for-profit in nature. The common thread is that church-based social enterprise seeks to meet the needs of its community with a sustainable (or more sustainable) financial model. While not identical in meaning, social enterprise relates to redemptive entrepreneurship in application. For example, a redemptive entrepreneur is usually engaging in social enterprise on the ground. See glossary for more on the various terms.

behavior for a governing body of a mainline denomination!). He told me that in the end it was the impact of our mission that persuaded them to invest in us. We had prepared comprehensive financial projections, played out worst-case scenarios, and hired lawyers to create extensive paperwork. All of that was important. As was the financial return we were providing them to continue their programming. But ultimately, it was the fact that in a typical decade we support the spiritual, emotional, and intellectual growth of almost ten thousand students. They made a true *impact* investment. It was the impact that mattered most.

Would they have made more money by keeping their $2.5 million in the stock and bond markets over the past seven years? Probably. But would that extra money have been worth the loss of a vibrant campus ministry at one of the largest universities in the country? No, it would not have. Their financial rate of return over those years from investment in a traditional portfolio would not have included the mission impact return we have generated in the lives of thousands of students. Jed Emerson, one of the early pioneers of impact investing, calls this the "blended value return." Blending the financial return on investment with the mission impact return on investment gives a much fuller picture of how well an investment is performing than only looking at the dollars generated. And the synod found their blended return on the Pres House investment to be high. For when our next refinance came around a few years ago, the synod renewed it for another seven-year period.

This impact investment was born of necessity. In fact, when the idea of approaching the synod for an investment came into focus for me in the middle of one of many sleepless nights, I had never even heard of the term "impact investing." I was just looking for a solution to a problem. We needed capital. And there is a lot of capital in the wider church system. I had heard of other examples of church entities lending to congregations, camps, and other organizations. But I had no idea there was a serious, and rapidly growing, area of investment called impact investing. It wasn't until I started considering how we could do more of this sort of thing in the church ecosystem that I discovered there are experts, books, conferences, and big players in this space called impact investing.

"Impact investing" has come to mean a particular kind of investing where money is proactively invested to produce social impact as well as financial returns. Emerson defines the term this way: "It is not simply invested, but directed capital seeking to be intentionally activated to explore various levels of financial performance with diverse forms of return while simultaneously addressing—and advancing solutions for—myriad social and environmental challenges."[6] Companies and social enterprises using impact investment return this blended value to investors in the form of both financial returns *and* social and environmental impact.

Impact investing is more than just negatively screening out "bad" investments that are deemed harmful. And it is not giving money away, as in philanthropy. Impact investing is somewhere in the middle—it is both/and. It is both an investment that generates financial return *and* an attempt to make an intentional, positive impact in the world with capital. Impact investments may produce a "market-rate" financial return alongside the social return. Or they may intentionally "give up" some financial return in order to make a larger social impact. The diagram below shows where impact investing fits on the spectrum.

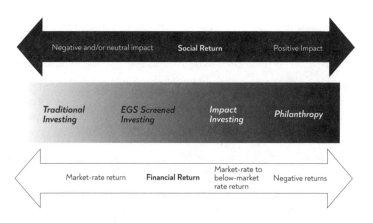

6. Jed Emerson, *The Purpose of Capital: Elements of Impact, Financial Flows, and Natural Being* (San Francisco: Blended Value, 2018), 32.

As I began learning more about what I had stumbled upon at Pres House, I found that impact investing is happening all over the place. The Global Impact Investing Network estimates that the worldwide impact-investing market is about $502 billion, managed by more than 1,340 organizations.[7] This number is rapidly changing, as the sector grows at more than 18 percent per year.[8] Investors include individuals, family offices, foundations, pensions funds—essentially anyone with capital to put to work for returns and impact. Investments can be in affordable housing, job creation, clean energy, microfinance, and so much more. It is not surprising that the sector is growing. A study as far back as 2011 found that 65 percent of investors want to achieve social impact from their investments, in addition to financial returns, and the Deloitte consulting firm found recently that 71 percent of millennials believe that "improving society" should be a top priority for business.[9] As J. P. Morgan stated in their overview of impact investing in 2010, "With increasing numbers of investors rejecting the notion that they face a binary choice between investing for maximum risk-adjusted returns or donating for a social purpose . . . we believe that impact investing will reveal itself to be one of the most powerful changes within the asset management industry in the years to come."[10]

Many foundations and funds have moved in this direction. The Nathan Cummings Foundation recently moved 100 percent of its $448 million endowment into impact investments.[11] The Russell

7. As of the end of 2018. Abhilash Mudaliar and Hannah Dithrich, *Sizing the Impact Investing Market* (n.p.: Global Impact Investing Network, 2019), https://thegiin.org/assets/Sizing%20the%20Impact%20Investing%20Market_webfile.pdf.

8. Women's Philanthropy Institute, *How Women and Men Approach Impact Investing*, Lilly Family School of Philanthropy, 2018, https://scholarworks.iupui.edu/bitstream/handle/1805/16229/Impact%20Investing%20Report%20FINAL.pdf.

9. Judith Rodin and Margot Brandenburg, *The Power of Impact Investing: Putting Markets to Work for Profit and Global Good* (Philadelphia: Wharton Digital, 2014), 31.

10. J. P. Morgan Chase Global Research, "Impact Investments: An Emerging Asset Class," November 29, 2010, https://thegiin.org/assets/documents/Impact%20Investments%20an%20Emerging%20Asset%20Class2.pdf.

11. The Nathan Cummings Foundation, https://nathancummings.org/ncf-commits-to-100-percent/.

Family Foundation recently outlined its four-year effort to move from 7 percent to almost 75 percent mission-aligned investments, with financial returns that beat market benchmarks by nearly 3 percent.[12] Hiromichi Mizuno, who oversees the $1.6 trillion Japan Government Pension Investment Fund, the world's largest public pension fund, is pushing for more impact investment in their portfolio.[13] Impact investing is here to stay.

## A New Economic Model for Ministry

In the church, impact investing, especially when combined with social enterprise, has the potential to fuel innovation and transformation in our communities where other forms of funding may not be adequate. At the same time that traditional sources of funding for ministry are shrinking in many quarters, there are new energy and interest in developing innovative forms of ministry and redemptive entrepreneurship that meet spiritual, emotional, and physical needs of people and communities. It is clear that both financially and programmatically, the church is selling something that fewer and fewer people want to "buy," and so, many of us are seeking innovative approaches to ministry and new expressions of what church looks like.

The trajectory of declining involvement that started in the 1960s at Pres House has continued throughout many parts of the church in the United States. In 2007 the Pew Research Center found that 78 percent of Americans identified as Christian and just 16 percent said they were religiously unaffiliated. By 2019, the first number had fallen to 65 percent and the second number had risen to 26 percent.[14]

12. The Russell Family Foundation, https://trff.org/impact-investments/.

13. Reshma Kapadia, "How the World's Largest Pension Manager Is Trying to Make ESG Investing More Popular," *Barron's*, April 12, 2019, https://www.barrons.com/articles/pension-manager-esg-impact-investing-51555020782/.

14. Pew Research Center, "In U.S., Decline of Christianity Continues at Rapid

Europe is significantly further ahead in this decline. I will not go into detail on the statistics or possible causes of this decline here because much has already been written on the subject. The bottom line is that fewer and fewer people are interested in joining an organization that primarily gathers for worship on Sunday mornings.

But that doesn't mean that churches and faith-based institutions have nothing to offer their communities. It just means that the expression of "church" in the world is changing. Congregations and other organizations in the system (seminaries, etc.) are experimenting with different ways of engaging their communities with the good news of Jesus Christ. Often these new forms of engagement look very different from Sunday morning worship. As Greg Jones correctly observes, "Most people are hungry for innovation. We are hungry for new ways of living and doing things that can chart better paths forward. We are hungry for innovation because we know we are facing challenges that are 'complex,' problems that are 'wicked.'"[15] There are people in the church tackling these wicked, complex problems with innovative solutions.

Redemptive entrepreneurs are working to solve some the most pressing wicked problems of today. And they are using creative expressions of social enterprise, both inside and outside of the church, to do so. Congregations are serving young entrepreneurs by converting fellowship halls into coworking spaces—drawing people into community who would never attend a worship service. They are organizing co-op grocery stores to address food deserts in their neighborhoods in a sustainable way. They are putting tiny houses on underutilized church property in order to provide homes for homeless neighbors. They are creating wine-tasting venues, lawn-care services, and fair-trade stores. Or they are building housing like we

Pace," October 17, 2019, https://www.pewforum.org/2019/10/17/in-u-s-decline-of-christianity-continues-at-rapid-pace/.

15. L. Gregory Jones, *Christian Social Innovation* (Nashville: Abingdon, 2016), 1.

did at Pres House—sometimes for students, sometimes for seniors, sometimes for lower-income neighbors who have been priced out of the market.

But these redemptive innovations require capital funding in order to get off the ground, and often at a different scale than the traditional grant- or donor-funding approach of the past.

Paul Bickley, research fellow at the Theos think tank in London, offers three essential elements to the development of faith-based social innovation: effective institutions that are the *engines* of social innovation; new kinds of leaders who become the *drivers* of this important work; and *fuel*—the money to fund social innovation on the ground. In looking at faith-based social innovation in the United Kingdom, Paul found that religious institutions struggled to access capital—the fuel to launch their projects. "Funding for religious social action is one of the main limitations on its growth."[16]

This was true for us at Pres House. Pres House was facing a bleak future. We had a very valuable and beautiful asset—property right in the heart of a large university. But a major capital infusion was needed to change the future of the organization. The historic landmark church building needed $2.5 million in restoration and repair just to keep functioning. A roof built to last fifty years had not been replaced seventy-five years later. And developing the parking lot into student housing required a significant capital investment. A typical donation or grant would not have been enough to transform the ministry and financial model of Pres House. We needed something different.

Let's say, hypothetically, that the synod kept their $2.5 million invested in traditional stocks and bonds and took a fairly standard 5 percent annual distribution from those invested funds. That would produce a return of $125,000 per year. And let's say they decided to donate every dollar of those earnings to Pres House in the form of

16. Paul Bickley, *Doing Good Better: The Case for Faith-Based Social Innovation* (London: Theos, 2017), 16.

a grant. That would have been great! That is a lot of money. Much more than a typical church grant. But $125,000 would not have been enough to help us build the Pres House Apartments. We needed a different kind of funding for this venture. We needed a much larger capital infusion to transform our organization, become sustainable, and influence thousands of lives. We needed the capital, not just the earnings. With that capital we have been able to produce spiritual, emotional, and intellectual returns in the lives of thousands of students and pay the synod almost $1 million in financial returns.

I love grants. I love philanthropy. But there are places and projects that need a different kind of financial model.

Impact investment from one church-related entity (the synod) into social enterprise created by another (Pres House) transformed two institutions and the lives of thousands of students. It created a sustainable financial model for fruitful ministry to flourish year after year. On a broader scale, the capital assets of the church, coupled with the creativity and human assets of entrepreneurs, can be brought together for remarkable outcomes. Impact investing in social enterprise creates enormous potential to transform lives in new and relevant ways and generate sustainable revenue. We are not broke.

2

## *The Way We've Always Done It*

A s our story at Pres House reveals, impact investing coupled with social enterprise has the potential to open up new forms of ministry while at the same time generating the financial resources necessary to carry out that ministry. So, surely this must be happening all over the place!

Alas, it is not. Even though the church has sometimes led important social movements in the past, we are well behind the curve in modern impact investing and social enterprise. Less than 3 percent of congregations have established separate social enterprises.[1] Several orders of nuns have been engaged in impact investing with their retirement funds for decades, but the practice in general has not taken off. Only 11 percent of faith-based investors surveyed by the Global Impact Investing Network engage in impact investing as part of their investment strategy.[2] Thirty-four percent of churches in the United States have an endowment.[3] But a survey of Presbyterian congrega-

1. Lake Institute on Faith and Giving, "The National Study of Congregations' Economic Practices," Indiana University Lilly Family School of Philanthropy, 2019, https://www.nscep.org/wp-content/uploads/2019/09/Lake_NSCEP_09162019-F -LR.pdf, 15.

2. Global Impact Investing Network, "Engaging Faith-Based Investors in Impact Investing," *Global Impact Investing Network Report*, January 2020, https://thegiin .org/assets/Engaging%20Faith-Based%20Investors%20in%20Impact%20Investing_ FINAL.pdf.

3. Lake Institute, "National Study," 16.

tions found that less than 1 percent were doing some kind of impact investing with their money.[4] According to one source, the Presbyterian Foundation has room to invest as much as 10 percent of funds held for the national church in impact funds and activities, but less than 2 percent actually are invested that way.[5] Wespath, the pension and investment fund of the United Methodist Church, engages in meaningful investing in affordable housing and community development. But those impact investments still only represent less than 4 percent of the $22 billion in assets that Wespath administers.[6] More disappointing, I was recently told by the CEO of a different major denominational pension fund that the fund "will never do impact investing."

While the synod investment in Pres House is an excellent example of the power church capital can have to transform lives and organizations, their $2.5 million investment was just a small part of the $17 million of capital we needed for this project. The rest came from outside the church in the form of tax-exempt bonds backed by a letter of credit from a regional bank. In other words, the majority of our financing came from conventional, commercial lending instruments. But I have to wonder, Why? With billions of dollars in the Presbyterian world alone, why is any of our debt financed by commercial banks? Why isn't there even $17 million of investment in the church to fund a church-based social enterprise that returns excellent financial and social-impact outcomes?

I will unpack some of the barriers and perils of impact investment in the church context in a later chapter. But first it is important to explore how church institutions have traditionally funded ministry and managed capital assets.

4. The PCUSA Clerk's Annual Questionnaire 2017, Faith Based Investing, prepared by Rob Fohr, March 2018.

5. From conversation with Rob Bullock, former vice president for marketing and communications at the Presbyterian Foundation.

6. From analysis of WESPATH portfolio and information at https://www.wespath.org/psp/.

The traditional model of church funding could be described as a "two-pocket" approach shared by many in the wider investment and philanthropic world. Money is made from one pocket via business, investing, or other forms of generating revenue. And then money is given away out of the second pocket in the form of philanthropy, donating, or almsgiving.

Historically the church has embraced this "two-pocket" approach to money in a couple of different ways. One is in voluntary giving from church members. Church members make money in their employment or business. Most of that money is used for living expenses and investments and so forth (taken out of pocket 1), and another, smaller, portion of that money is given to the church (taken out of pocket 2). James Hudnut-Beumler explores the evolution of funding Protestant churches in the United States in his recent book *In Pursuit of the Almighty's Dollar: A History of Money and American Protestantism*. In the earliest days of Protestant church development in the United States, funding came in the form of state support, renting pews to members, and other sources of revenue. But by the mid-nineteenth century, funding had evolved to be primarily voluntary giving from members.

In 1878 C. P. Jennings wrote that tithing from individuals was the only proper way to sustain the church and pay pastors and that no other forms of income should be used.[7] Similarly, Alexander Hogshead insisted that the church should not be supported by modern business schemes and that member giving was the only faithful way to support it.[8] In this model, funds are generated by members and then given away for the church to use. This model, of course, continues today. Religious organizations receive the most charitable support of any kind of organization in the United States. In 2017, 31 percent of $410 billion of charitable support went to religious organizations. Education received

7. James Hudnut-Beumler, *In Pursuit of the Almighty's Dollar: A History of Money and American Protestantism* (Chapel Hill: University of North Carolina Press, 2007), 51.

8. Hudnut-Beumler, *In Pursuit of the Almighty's Dollar*, 54.

the next highest amount at 14 percent.[9] Eighty-one percent of congregational revenue comes from individual donations, and 78 percent of that giving occurs during worship services, or, in other words, through "passing the plate," either literally or via online giving.[10]

While the majority of church support has come from member contributions in the past couple of hundred years, churches also established endowments early on.[11] Those endowments were invested so as to produce financial returns that would provide funding for mission and ministry. That practice continues today. There are billions of dollars of invested endowment assets in my denomination of ordination alone, the PCUSA. My seminary alma mater, Princeton Theological Seminary, has a roughly $1 billion endowment. One institution. As already noted, the ICCR network of religious investors manages more than $400 billion in assets. When we talk about declining funding in some church networks, we are not being entirely accurate. There may be declining giving, but there are huge storehouses of invested money in even the most struggling denominations.

Most of this invested endowment money has also functioned in a "two-pocket" approach. Money is invested out of one pocket to make more money. Then the earnings from that investment are used for operating the church or given away for mission.

The vast majority of "religious" invested assets are invested in market instruments like the stock and bond markets. We hand almost all our assets over to Mark Zuckerberg and others to grow their business in exchange for some earnings back. The top holdings of the Presbyterian New Covenant Fund are Amazon, Apple, Alphabet (Google's parent company), and Facebook.[12]

We give the bulk of our capital to those companies and others like

9. Charity Navigator Giving Statistics, accessed July 13, 2020, https://www.charitynavigator.org/index.cfm?bay=content.view&cpid=42.

10. Lake Institute, "National Study," 14, 17.

11. Hudnut-Beumler, *In Pursuit of the Almighty's Dollar*, 10.

12. From conversation with Paul Grier, vice president of project regeneration, Presbyterian Foundation.

them. They put our capital to work and use it to grow their business. Jeff Bezos, the richest man in the world, uses our money to design the next Alexa, sell it on Amazon, and then give us a little bit back in the form of dividends or appreciated stock value. Tim Cook uses our money to design the Apple Watch, purchase the raw materials, build watches, sell them, and then give us a little bit back in the form of dividends or appreciated stock value. That is how the system works, we are told. "That is how we've always done it," we hear—a familiar refrain in many church institutions.

Kevin Jones, one of the founders of Social Capital Markets (SO-CAP), a premier conference on impact investing, tells a story about meeting Bill Gates, who described his philanthropic giving in "two-pocket" terms. Jones recounts:

> SOCAP, the world's largest impact investing and social enterprise conference, was born in Bill Gates' office. We wanted to invest in a fair-trade coffee company led by someone who'd been a direct report of his, so our entrepreneur managed to get an appointment to meet him in his office. For sixteen seconds. That's when Gates stood up and said "Stop. You have to understand, I have two pockets, one I put my investment dollars in, and I want to put all the money in the world there. I have another, smaller pocket I put some money in to do good. If you say there is a connection between those you have to leave. I can't hear it." We got kicked out of two other billionaires' offices with the pitch that you could invest seriously with the goals of philanthropy.[13]

Jed Emerson and Antony Bugg-Levine explain that this "'bifur-cated' world is built on two fundamental beliefs: that the only pur-

---

13. Kevin Jones, "How SOCAP Changed 'Two Pocket Thinking,'" *Transform*, July 8, 2019, https://thetransformseries.net/2019/07/08/how-socap-changed-two -pocket-thinking/.

pose of investing is to make money and that the only way to solve social and environmental challenges is to donate money to charities or wait for government to act."[14] Investing in those companies produces a nice return on our money—during most years at least. Sometimes we then give away the earnings we receive for mission. More often we use it to keep our churches and institutions open. Sometimes we just put it back into our endowments and foundations. In almost all cases we hope to make as much as we can in our investment pocket so we have more to spend out of our other pocket.

US foundations are required by the IRS to give away 5 percent of their assets each year. The rest of their assets can remain invested however they would like. This means that as much as 95 percent of their money could be used in direct contradiction with their mission, depending on their investment choices. While the percentages may be a little different for church institutions that are not technically foundations according to IRS code, many follow a similar pattern. Only a small fraction of total foundation assets are put to work directly in the communities and lives of the people they serve, while the vast majority spend their nights with Mark Zuckerberg and their days with Jeff Bezos.

We are told that the best place to earn the highest financial return at the lowest risk is in the S&P 500 index and other conventional investment options. We aren't confident that the local social entrepreneur is going to be able to give us the 9 percent annual return we expect Mark Zuckerberg to provide. So we put our money to bed in Silicon Valley and big energy. It turns out that the assumption that impact investing is a poor financial decision is not true. As Morgan Simon notes in her book *Real Impact*, "Study after study has shown that impact investments have been able to *outperform* the market with

14. Alex Goldmark, "Social Impact Investing: It's Not Wall Street as Usual," *Good*, October 21, 2011, https://www.good.is/articles/social-impact-investing-it-s-not-wall -street-as-usual.

lower levels of volatility."[15] As some in impact investing have said, it is possible to "do good and do well."

I am pleased and encouraged that impact investing can in some cases produce a strong financial return. It certainly does for the Synod of Lakes and Prairies and their investment in our property and mission at Pres House. It makes sense that treating workers well, contributing to society, and running an ethical business can also be profitable. Impact investing cannot be dismissed out of hand as a bad financial decision. But comparing the rate of return of investments is not the purpose of my exploration here. If making money from our money was the "purpose of capital," to borrow the title from Jed Emerson's recent book, then I could stop right here. We could research the risk-adjusted rate of return of impact investments and compare it to market investments, then make the case that our money would do better in impact investments, place our money there, and move on. While this would be an improvement over how we handle our capital currently, it is still missing the point.

The question I really want to wrestle with goes much deeper than financial performance. The real question we should be considering in the church is this: *What is the purpose of our capital?* What is the purpose of the money and property that the church owns? Is it to make more money? Or is it something else?

15. Morgan Simon, *Real Impact: The New Economics of Social Change* (New York: Nation Books, 2017), 35.

# 3

## *Highest and Best Use—Bigger Barns or Something Else?*

When I started as copastor at Pres House sixteen years ago, I had a bachelor's degree in psychology and a master of divinity degree. I had learned how to read Greek and Hebrew (sort of!), how to think theologically, and how to deliver a passable sermon. But much of my actual day-to-day work involved managing employees, understanding complex financing arrangements, reading and signing contracts, developing a marketing strategy, and other aspects of running a multimillion-dollar-per-year social business. Thankfully I love to learn new things. And I was good at asking for help from people who know more than I. So for twelve years I learned the business on the job. But in 2015 I decided I needed a deeper knowledge of business practices and to think not only theologically but also with business in mind. While many of my seminary classmates were getting PhDs and DMin degrees, I went back to school for an MBA (master of business administration).

I loved it. I loved learning and talking about running business well. Don't be mistaken—I also have a healthy skepticism of business. I do not believe in unfettered capital markets. But I am also not afraid of business. Running the business of mission well can have a profound positive impact. It is not enough for me to dream and vision, or to write and preach. For change to happen in lives and communities, action must also be taken. And business done right can lead to transformative action.

I am also not opposed to organizations seeking to make money. I resonate with Gilbert Monks, who a century ago lamented that clergy had too little interest in money and the business affairs of the world. He encouraged clergy to try new things and engage in their work in a businesslike fashion.[1] My experience at Pres House has shown me that effectively leveraging financial resources can have a profound positive effect on mission and ministry. And yet the church has at times adopted the worst practices of business without critique while ignoring some of the best practices of business that would help us serve our communities.

One of the underlying concepts that comes up in business school is that the purpose of capital is to seek its "highest and best use." In conventional investing, that has meant finding the highest rate of return with the lowest risk and putting our money there so it can grow as rapidly and as risk-free as possible. As Jed Emerson explains, "Our traditional understanding of the purpose of capital is to use it as a tool by which we hope to increase and grow its amount in our portfolio."[2]

But is that really the purpose of capital? Is that actually the highest and best use for our money? Is growth for growth's sake good? Not always. Cancer grows just to grow—and then kills us.[3] Growth is not the same as creating value. Is the capital in the church truly creating value? "We do not have to accept the definition of capital's purpose as developed in the last four centuries and which we have enthusiastically bought from Wall Street's firms of finance. . . . At its core the notion of capital is itself a social construct, and not an objective rule

---

1. James Hudnut-Beumler, *In Pursuit of the Almighty's Dollar: A History of Money and American Protestantism* (Chapel Hill: University of North Carolina Press, 2007), 59.

2. Jed Emerson, *The Purpose of Capital: Elements of Impact, Financial Flows, and Natural Being* (San Francisco: Blended Value, 2018), 37.

3. Emerson, *The Purpose of Capital*, 249.

of law operating beyond our societal bounds."[4] It is our money. We can handle it however we want to.

No, that is not accurate. It is not our money. It is *God's* money. And therefore, we should think carefully about how we put God's money to work. Growing the money by whatever means possible may not be the best way to use what God has given us. Here I am drawn to Scripture, and particularly the parable of the rich fool, for, as Walter Brueggemann affirms, "Economics is a core preoccupation of the biblical tradition."[5]

The parable of the rich fool found in Luke 12 was prompted by a question. Jesus is talking to a crowd when someone calls out, "Teacher, tell my brother to divide the family inheritance with me." According to Judaic inheritance practices, an older brother would receive two-thirds of an inheritance while the younger would receive one-third.[6] This younger brother sees Jesus as a potential advocate who will help him get more from his brother. He probably doesn't expect to hear the answer Jesus then gives.

"Take care!" Jesus says. "Be on your guard against all kinds of greed; for one's life does not consist in the abundance of possessions." The word "greed" in the original Greek could also be translated "yearning for increase."[7] Instead of addressing the question of the man's claim on his father's wealth, Jesus uses the opportunity to teach the crowd about money. And he begins by warning the crowd to be wary of continually yearning for increase. Jesus then tells a story that speaks to those of us who have resources today just as powerfully as it did to those who heard it originally.

---

4. Emerson, *The Purpose of Capital*, 2.

5. Walter Brueggemann, *Money and Possessions* (Louisville: Westminster John Knox, 2016), xix.

6. Richard P. Carlson, "Feasting on the Word—Year C, Volume 3: Pentecost and Season after Pentecost 1 (Propers 3–16)," in *Feasting on the Word: Preaching the Revised Common Lectionary* (Louisville: Westminster John Knox, 2010).

7. Brueggemann, *Money and Possessions*, 192.

There is a rich man. His wealth is measured in land and the quantity of crops that land produces. And this man's land produces abundantly. In fact, it produces so much that he can't find anywhere to store all the grain. The language Jesus uses here is instructive—the *land* produces abundantly. Not "the man works hard" or the "man is brilliant and got rich" or "the man pulls himself up by his bootstraps." No, the land produces abundantly. He does not simply fill his barns by himself. He is helped into his wealth.

Furthermore, when God comes to the rich man at the end of the story to demand his life back, the language God uses is that of a person recalling a loan. Even the man's very life is a loan from God. Everything the man has, including his very life, is given or loaned to him by God. For Brueggemann, this suggests that "Money and possessions belong to God and are held in trust by human persons in community."[8]

But does the rich man acknowledge this? Is he grateful to God for his life and all he has been entrusted with? Does he recognize that he is simply a steward of land and resources that are not his to own? No. He doesn't. The land produced abundantly in verse 16, but by verse 17 those riches have become "*my* crops." The man immediately starts making plans to store "*my* grain" and "*my* goods." The rich man takes full ownership of what is not his to own.

This lack of perspective is all around us. The myth of the "self-made" person is deeply embedded in the American psyche. The myth goes like this: We all start out with a level playing field, and if we just work hard enough and are smart enough, we can get ahead. Anyone can be a millionaire. Anyone can pull himself or herself up by the bootstraps. But this myth is just that—a myth. The United States actually scores very low on social mobility—the measure of how easily people can move from poverty to wealth across generations. We score lower than almost all other developed countries.[9] It turns out

8. Brueggemann, *Money and Possessions*, 4.

9. Elise Gould, "U.S. Lags behind Peer Countries in Mobility," *Economic Policy*

that where people end up is mostly a result of where they started and factors outside of their control. And social mobility is getting worse. Absolute mobility declined for recent birth cohorts; barely half the men and women born in the 1980s were upwardly mobile compared with two-thirds of those born in the 1940s.[10] Just as literally pulling yourself up by your bootstraps is physically impossible, metaphorically pulling yourself up by your bootstraps is almost as difficult. I know this is true in my life. My parents were well educated and, by worldwide standards at least, rich. I had the opportunity to go to good schools as a child, to travel around the world, and to visit museums on weekends. I had a stable place to live and enough food on the table every day. Studies show that the more books a child has in the home growing up, the higher the child's educational outcomes will be.[11] Well, I grew up with lots of books. And I received all these hand-ups without any work of my own. They were given to me. The land I was born into produced abundantly.

As an adult, I am still getting hand-ups. I have had the privilege to go to a good college and multiple graduate schools. As a white man living in a country that was founded upon the genocide of native people and built on the backs of enslaved Africans, I still benefit from an economic system that was created to enrich white men. I have never had to worry about redlining and other forms of housing discrimination that affect people of color, so I have always been able to get a loan and buy a home in a neighborhood I wanted to. And as a homeowner, I benefit from a massive $61 billion government handout—the mortgage interest tax deduction. The ability to deduct

*Institute*, October 10, 2012, https://www.epi.org/publication/usa-lags-peer-countries -mobility/.

10. Michael Hout, "Americans' Occupational Status Reflects the Status of Both of Their Parents," *Proceedings of the National Academy of Sciences* 115, no. 38 (September 18, 2018): 9527–32, https://doi.org/10.1073/pnas.1802508115.

11. Joanna Sikora, M. D. R. Evans, and Jonathan Kelley, "Scholarly Culture: How Books in Adolescence Enhance Adult Literacy, Numeracy and Technology Skills in 31 Societies," *Social Science Research* 77 (January 2019).

mortgage interest payments on my home from my taxes is a massive social welfare program for people who can afford to own homes. It is welfare for the rich. The land I've been given, and that people who look like me have taken from others, has produced abundantly.

It is very easy to fall into the trap of the rich fool who took all the credit and failed to see this reality. I am grateful that God has used friends, teachers, prophets, and my partner, Erica, to strip the scales from my eyes over many years and help me see more clearly. Land that I have access to has produced abundantly. Deeply rooted systemic racism and white supremacy have afforded me opportunities, wealth, and freedoms that many Americans, including my own biracial children, do not fully share. For this reality, the ways I perpetuate it, and how my own racism rears its ugly head, I am deeply sorry. I must be honest about this reality as the starting point for repentance and renewal.

The rich fool lacked perspective. He laid claim to goods that were not his to own. That was his first big mistake. His second mistake was to think only of himself. When he experiences success, the rich man can only see the *problem* of storing his riches for himself rather than the *responsibility* he has to steward his excess differently. "Where am I going to store all my extra stuff?" he cries. He decides to tear down his barns and build larger ones in order to store all his grain. It is like when I've gone shopping for a new bookcase or storage tote or a bigger house in order to store my growing supply of stuff. When I first left college, I could move everything I owned in a small two-door car. Now I would have to hire a full-size truck to move it all. Building more storage seems like a good solution for the rich man. Make more room to store more stuff so he can have more than enough far into the future.

But, why didn't he store some of that grain in the mouths of hungry people? And what about today? He was saving up for some future day. What about the needs all around him today?

The problem of too much stuff was—is—a classic "first-world problem." Not a problem at all. But an opportunity. The rich man had an opportunity to open his eyes to the needs of others around him and to redistribute some of the abundance. He had a responsibility to do something about the injustice and inequality of having so much he didn't know what to do with it while others struggled just to survive. He had the chance to not just store up treasure for himself but be rich toward God.

"You fool," God says to him. "I am going to recall the loan that is your life tonight."

Suddenly the man is left with nothing: no goods, no grain, no barns, not even his life. There are no barns—and no banks—in heaven. The plush life he had tried to secure for himself vanishes. What appeared to be wise stewardship of his surplus turned out to be foolish. Jesus closes the story with a simple statement: "So it is with those who store up treasures for themselves but are not rich toward God." The rich man experienced exactly what Jesus warned his disciples about a few chapters earlier in Luke: "What does it profit them if they gain the whole world, but lose or forfeit themselves?"[12]

12. Luke 9:25. Unless otherwise indicated, all biblical quotations in this book come from the New Revised Standard Version.

4

*Open the Barns, Don't Build More*

The rich fool in Jesus's parable lost himself by losing his way with money. I believe he missed two key principles about interacting with money that we should recall in any discussion about investment and capital: (1) everything we have is on loan to us from God, and (2) we need to control money rather than let it control us. These two principles are an invitation to live differently and not repeat the mistakes of our barn-building ancestor.

### Everything We Have Is a Gift (Loan) from God

The rich fool failed to see that all that he had was on loan to him from God. Even his very life. As the psalmist sings, "The earth is the LORD's and all that is in it."[1] The resources that we have, as individuals and institutions, are loaned to us by God for us to put to good use while we have the opportunity. They are not "ours." The idea "that possessions are gifts and not achievements or accomplishments is a decisive check in biblical faith on any temptation to imagine self-sufficiency or autonomy and contradicts the marketplace that assumes there are no handouts and everything received is earned."[2]

1. Ps. 24:1.
2. Walter Brueggemann, *Money and Possessions* (Louisville: Westminster John Knox, 2016), 2.

Emerson writes, "While one may temporarily own capital, it is not in its essence yours. . . . The purpose of money may, in the end, have more to do with your managing that wealth on behalf of the Other than on behalf of your Self."[3]

This is not a new idea. But it is one we need to reclaim. In 1891 Josiah Strong wrote a chapter about money in his best-selling book from the time, *Our Country*. In that chapter he highlighted the power of money and property to solve the social problems of the day (much as I am doing here today). He also made the important claim that Christians are "simply trustees or managers of God's property."[4] In a 1914 book about stewardship in the church, Harvey Reeves Calkin made a distinction between ownership and possession.[5] God owns. Humans just possess for the time being. The vital truth that everything we have is on loan from God is bedrock to living a life rich toward God and not constantly yearning for increase.

Saint Ambrose, drawing upon stories of the early church in Acts, wrote, "For nature generously supplies everything for everyone in common. God ordained everything to be produced to provide food for everyone in common; his plan was that the earth should be as it were, the common possession of us all. Nature produced common rights, then, it is usurping greed that has established private rights."[6] As a dual citizen of Britain and the United States, born in the United States to immigrant parents from the United Kingdom, I have always found the practice of public footpaths in England to be refreshing. When going for a walk in the English countryside, one can hike for miles on public paths that wind their way through private land. The

---

3. Jed Emerson, *The Purpose of Capital: Elements of Impact, Financial Flows, and Natural Being* (San Francisco: Blended Value, 2018), 43.

4. James Hudnut-Beumler, *In Pursuit of the Almighty's Dollar: A History of Money and American Protestantism* (Chapel Hill: University of North Carolina Press, 2007), 62.

5. Cited in Hudnut-Beumler, *In Pursuit of the Almighty's Dollar*, 67.

6. Emerson, *The Purpose of Capital*, 207.

idea is to provide access to all people to the countryside that would otherwise be off-limits due to private ownership of land.

This is such a contrast to an experience I had trying to access a national forest in California a number of years ago. A friend and I set off one weekend to backpack around some enticing lakes in the mountains of northern California. We picked up provisions in Shasta City and then headed out into the wilderness. After a couple of wrong turns, we were on the right track, making our way up narrow rocky roads into the backcountry. Our excitement for the trip was building, the sun was shining, life was looking good. And then we ran into a gate. The road we were driving on was blocked by a huge metal pole serving as a gate. We stopped and got out to take a look. On the gate was a sign that read Private Land. No Trespassing. Below that was posted a reference to the part of California state law that protects private land from trespassers.

This seemed absurd. The public trailhead was just about a half mile farther up the road and was the only way into the lakes that we had been dreaming about visiting for weeks. So we looked at each other and decided to take a chance and keep going. We thought if we could just get through the little piece of private property quickly, no one would notice and we'd be on our way to a great trip. I opened the gate, my friend drove the truck through, I closed it behind us, and we kept going—a little faster than before. We bumped along for another couple of minutes until we came around the bend and saw . . . another gate. Only this time it was covered in huge bright signs. It said, "This is private property! You are being watched on video. No trespassing. You will be sorry if you keep going," and other ominous threats. Needless to say, at that point we turned around. While we later found a different spot to hike and camp, we never did make it to those lakes.

This obsession with private ownership and need to protect what we have from others is a powerful force in the culture and the founding of the United States. Where First Nations people shared access to land, those who came to our shores from Europe immediately set about taking the land for private ownership. Christopher Columbus remarked that the First Nations people live "without covetousness of another man's goods."[7] This sounds remarkably like the vision of the early Christian church: "Now the whole group of those who believed were of one heart and soul, and no one claimed private ownership of any possessions, but everything they owned was held in common."[8] A lack of covetousness, and sharing of resources for all, was soon replaced in America by manifest destiny and a systematic conquering of people and lands. What God had provided became "*my* grain" and "*my* goods."

But this does not have to be the way we live.

Shifting our mind-set from a view that our resources and capital are ours and ours alone to an understanding that all we have is on loan from God opens up many new opportunities and possibilities for how to use our capital. If the property of the church is God's, what would God want us to do with it? If the endowment of a church is God's, how would God want that capital to be put to work? If the money invested in denominational pension funds is God's and not ours, how might that impact the way we invest those funds? Perhaps instead of building larger and larger barns to hold more of "our" assets, we could open up those barns and put God's resources to work in the world.

Author and speaker Shane Claiborne tells a story about visiting Mother Teresa in Calcutta, India. One of his regular duties was to help the sisters put on a meal for some very poor children. One particular day was the birthday of a young boy who had come for the meal. Shane snuck out and bought the boy an ice-cream cone as a special treat—something the boy had likely rarely, if ever, tasted before.

7. Quoted in Emerson, *The Purpose of Capital*, 207.
8. Acts 4:32.

"Happy birthday, kid," whispered Shane. "Now keep this quiet because I don't have enough money to buy one for everybody else."

What did the birthday boy do? He immediately yelled out, "Hey everyone! We have ice cream!"

The ensuing stampede had Shane running for cover and dreading a sea of disappointed faces. But the birthday boy's next announcement turned the tide. "Now, listen up. We have only one cone, so we all get one lick."

The kids formed a line, at which point the birthday boy proceeded to share his cone with all the others. Who was the last person to get a lick? The birthday boy himself. For Shane, this experience revealed what he calls the secret of Jesus: the best thing to do, with the best things in life, is to give them away.[9]

## Control Money—Don't Let Money Control You

The rich fool lived his life in fear of not having enough even though he had plenty. Instead of sharing from his abundance, he tried to gather it all up for the future. A future that would never come. This mind-set of scarcity has infected American people and churches. Lynne Twist observes, "Everyone is interested in money, and almost all of us feel a chronic concern, or even fear, that we will never really have enough or be able to keep enough of it."[10] This is as true for those who have far more money than they can spend in a lifetime as it is for those who truly live in need.

Twist calls out this scarcity mind-set as a dangerous and life-

9. Shane Claiborne shared this story while speaking to hundreds of college students at Pres House on February 26, 2015. It is also recounted in a blog post by Claiborne: "A Radical Redistribution of Love," *KolbeTimes*, April 11, 2019, https://www.kolbetimes.com/radical-redistribution-of-love/.

10. Lynne Twist, *The Soul of Money: Transforming Your Relationship with Money and Life* (New York: Norton, 2017), 6.

draining lie built upon three pervasive myths: (1) There is not enough. (2) More is better. (3) That's just the way it is.[11] These lies have made their way into our personal psyche, and I believe they have replicated like a virus in the church.

First, we think there is not enough. We might ask ourselves, enough for what? But we don't usually get to that question. We simply believe there is never enough. No matter how much we have, there is still never enough. The power of Michael Mather's story about Broadway United Methodist Church in Indianapolis is that he was able to see through the lie that there wasn't enough in his community. Where others saw scarcity, he was able to see that their community did have something. Lots of somethings, in fact. The same is true in the finances of the larger church. There are certainly churches that have very little to work with, especially since the economic downturn caused by the COVID-19 pandemic. But other institutions in the church ecosystem have more than enough. Recall the $400 billion of investments held by church institutions and the incredible amount of church property located in almost every corner of this country. When I hear folks in the church say there isn't enough money to do *x*, *y*, or *z*, I want to say (in the kindest way possible), "That is a lie." It is a perpetuation of the lie of scarcity. There is enough. We just need to think differently about how we use what we do have.

Second, we are drawn to the myth that more is always better. This is "the logical response if you fear there's not enough, but 'more is better' drives a competitive culture of accumulation, acquisition, and greed that only heightens fears and quickens the pace of the race."[12] When we step back from this myth, we know instinctively that more is not always better and that constantly seeking more leaves us, our communities, and our environment exhausted and pillaged. A well-

11. Twist, *The Soul of Money*, 48–54.
12. Twist, *The Soul of Money*, 50.

known study out of Princeton University found that people were no happier making a $10 million salary than they were making $75,000.[13] In fact, making anything above $75,000 provided no increase in happiness. More is not always better. There is a point of enough. Even Andrew Carnegie, the late nineteenth-century businessman and very rich man, said, "The amassing of wealth is one of the worst species of idolatry."[14]

The endless quest for more has become perhaps the most powerful and pervasive "religion" in America today. Yuval Noah Harari observes that previous religious and ethical systems asked followers to restrain their selfish interests. But the capitalist-consumerist religion that has taken over American life today does just the opposite. Followers are promised paradise if they fuel their greed, give in to all cravings, and constantly buy more. Ironically and tragically, "This is the first religion in history whose followers actually do what they are asked to do."[15]

Most of us understand intuitively that constantly seeking more is not a healthy way to live. We talk about balance and gratitude. But cultivating gratitude and simplicity is difficult when the entire market economy that we live within in the United States is fueled by an endless drive for more, more, more. Our market economy grows when we produce and buy more. It is really as simple as that. Without more production, without more spending, without more consumption, there is no growth.

There is perhaps no starker example of how this works than what Americans were asked to do after the tragedy of September 11, 2001:

13. Daniel Kahneman and Angus Deaton, "High Income Improves Evaluation of Life but Not Emotional Well-being," *Proceedings of the National Academy of Sciences* 107, no. 38 (September 21, 2010): 16489–93.

14. Quoted by John Fullerton, "A 'Gospel of Wealth' for the 21st Century," in *Slow Investing*, ed. John Bloom (Phoenixville, PA: Lilipoh Publishing, 2011), 41.

15. Yuval Noah Harari, *Sapiens: A Brief History of Humankind* (New York: Harper Perennial, 2015), 349.

go shopping. I will never forget that one of the primary invitations of American patriotism suggested by President Bush was for us all to go shopping. For by spending more we would keep the economy growing, and a growing economy was supposed to somehow protect us from those who wished us harm.

The COVID-19 pandemic also made this reality abundantly clear. Within days of learning that the coronavirus was spreading, communities began shutting down. By the end of March 2020, more than one hundred countries had instituted a full or partial lockdown in which billions of citizens were asked to stay in their homes and minimize interaction. Schools, universities, shops, factories, and workplaces closed on an unprecedented scale. The economic impact was devastating. In less than two months, thirty-three million Americans had filed for unemployment. A year that began with projections for broad economic growth and the highest level ever reached by the US stock market suddenly turned into a year that will be remembered for generations as the fastest and deepest recession ever to hit the world. When we stop shopping, the system falls apart.

The importance of endless consumption on the overall economy is one of the reasons that economic stimulus packages during recessions usually include tax rebates or payroll tax relief—because the assumption is that if more money can be put in the hands of people who will spend it, then as a nation we can spend our way out of trouble. And there is some truth to the way this works. More spending does increase GDP (gross domestic product)—a common measure of economic strength of a nation. GDP in the United States has grown from $744 billion in 1965 to $21.4 trillion in 2019.[16]

But a number of far less desirable measures have also grown during that time period. Inequality in wealth and income in the United States has reached its highest level in fifty years. Three individuals, Jeff Bezos, Bill Gates of Microsoft, and investor Warren Buffett, own

16. https://data.worldbank.org/indicator/NY.GDP.MKTP.CD?locations=US.

more of our nation's wealth than the bottom 50 percent of all Americans combined.[17] Those three people own more than do 160 million other Americans, most of whom don't have enough emergency savings to cover three months of expenses.[18] For every one hundred dollars in white family wealth, Black families hold just five dollars.[19] Even though markets operate with an implicit assumption that more is always better, it is abundantly clear that "not all populations have benefited equally from the expansion of markets."[20]

This inequality comes with costs. My father, Ronald Elsdon, has explored the implications of inequality in our society and suggested that business has a key role to play in solving these problems. He writes, "There is growing evidence that inequality in a society brings many social ills, which include lowered educational performance among children, reduced life expectancy, higher infant mortality, more obesity, increased crime, lower levels of trust, and less social mobility."[21] And he raises a provocative question, especially as we move into a post-COVID world and have an opportunity to rethink the way it has always been done:

17. Chuck Collins and Josh Hoxie, "Billionaire Bonanza," *Inequality.org.*, 2017, https://inequality.org/wp-content/uploads/2017/11/BILLIONAIRE-BONANZA -2017-Embargoed.pdf.

18. Kim Parker, Juliana Menasce Horowitz, and Anna Brown, "About Half of Lower-Income Americans Report Household Job or Wage Loss Due to COVID-19," Pew Research Center, April 21, 2020, https://www.pewsocialtrends.org/2020/04/21 /about-half-of-lower-income-americans-report-household-job-or-wage-loss-due-to -covid-19/.

19. Emily Badger, "Whites Have Huge Wealth Edge over Blacks (but Don't Know It)," *New York Times*, September 18, 2017, https://www.nytimes.com/interactive/2017 /09/18/upshot/black-white-wealth-gap-perceptions.html.

20. Rebecca Blank and William McGurn, *Is the Market Moral? A Dialogue on Religion, Economics, and Justice* (Washington, DC: Brookings Institution Press, 2004), 39.

21. Ron Elsdon, ed., *Business Behaving Well: Social Responsibility, from Learning to Doing* (Dulles, VA: Potomac Books, 2013), 2.

Over the past forty years, the United States has moved from a level of inequality similar to other developed countries to a level of inequality today that mirrors developing countries still trying to build their economies. This raises serious questions about the ability of our society to maintain its current level of prosperity if the level of inequality were to stay the same or increase. A critical question is, where would we like our society to move in the future? Is it to move toward further inequality and economic and social deprivation, or to greater equality and the benefit that brings?[22]

The myths that "there is not enough" and that "more is better" could be described in starker terms. The first myth is rooted in fear. We are afraid that there is not enough. The second is rooted in greed: we are continually greedy for more. To a great extent, our market economy is driven by these two powerful forces—fear and greed.

Churches and institutions fall victim to these same two dangers of fear and greed. We operate out of fear for the future. That there will not be enough. As Greg Jones writes, one of the biggest barriers to innovation in the church is that "we have turned inward and been shaped more by fear than by hope."[23] So we store up whatever we can in the biggest barns we can find. And we get greedy—always seeking more. More people. More pledges. More buildings. More programs. Striving to be relevant, to connect and serve people meaningfully, and to grow in breadth and depth are not bad things, but if *more* becomes the primary goal, there will never be enough.

There is a way in which we simultaneously don't take money seriously enough as a force in our world, as a driver of our faith, and

22. Elsdon, *Business Behaving Well*, 5.
23. L. Gregory Jones, *Christian Social Innovation* (Nashville: Abingdon, 2016), 8.

give it too much control in our lives and don't keep it in its place. We have let money, our worries about it, our desire to increase it or retain it, control us—our decisions, our plans, our future, our identity. It is time for us to uproot "the sacred character" of money and "bring money back to its role as a material instrument."[24] It is just a tool. Let us put money back in its rightful place, as a tool for us to control and not a force exerting control over us.

### How Much Is Enough?

For the first five years of operations at Pres House, we ran a negative budget. Like a Silicon Valley start-up, we spent more money each year than we brought in. Some of that was endowment money saved from earlier days. Some was borrowed money. We spent down half of a roughly $1 million endowment in order to get up and running. But eventually we moved into the black at the end of a fiscal year. We had brought in more money than we spent. Hurray! Since then we've been prudently working to save money in good years as a way of mitigating the major risks of potential interest rate increases and possible rental vacancy, both of which have happened over the years. It would take only one really bad year on either of those fronts for us to face significant financial difficulty.

But we have to ask ourselves, how much is too much to save? How much is enough? Pres House does not exist as an organization to build more barns in a huge endowment; we exist to welcome students with the love and grace of God. We do not exist to eliminate all risk by saving so much that nothing can touch us; we exist to help students stay sober in school and experience wellness in community. And so we have to work actively and consciously against the traps of

---

24. Jacques Ellul, quoted in Brueggemann, *Money and Possessions*, 195.

fear and greed in order to operate not out of a sense of scarcity but out of gratitude for opportunity.

That is the challenge for all of us and our organizations—to set aside fear and greed and live differently. Even though it is difficult, we *can* live differently. It is my hope for my life, and for the church, to live in such a way that we control money rather than let it control us. The lie of scarcity does not have to be the way it is. We can wrestle that lie to the ground and live differently. Lynne Twist's third myth of scarcity is that all this fear and greed is just the way it is and there is no other way to live. We justify the rat race for more by telling ourselves, "that is the way capitalism works," "grow or die," and "it has always been this way." We accept the traditional investment advice to seek the highest rate of return at the lowest risk because "that is what people do" and "that is how the system works."

But this is a particularly dangerous view for Christians and the church to adopt. "Among people of faith, self-interest is not an adequate principle for living. We are called to be other-interested as well as self-interested."[25] For God turns "the way things are" upside down. God loves the unlovable, gives sight to the blind, frees the one in bondage, meets violence with peace, and invites us to live differently. Immediately after telling the story of the rich fool, Jesus invites the disciples to "withdraw from the world of fear" and not be anxious about their lives.[26] Jesus reminds them that, like the lilies of the field and the birds of the air, they have enough. They are "not to be preoccupied with scarcity, and are not to be propelled by worry."[27]

I still think we need to aim for the highest and best use of capital. We just need to expand the definition of what that means. It is up to us to define the purpose of our capital—our own personal assets and the

---

25. Blank and McGurn, *Is the Market Moral?*, 23.

26. Brueggemann, *Money and Possessions*, 193.

27. Brueggemann, *Money and Possessions*, 193.

assets of our churches and institutions. Let us not allow that purpose to be defined by Wall Street and investment advisers. Let us not let fear of scarcity drive our decision making, or simply fall back into the way it has always been done. As University of Wisconsin–Madison chancellor and economist Rebecca Blank puts it, "As Christians, we cannot view all choices as morally neutral. Some choices lead us closer to God and some turn us away."[28] We do not need to continue to build bigger barns as a way to manage our anxiety about the future, or invest for the highest financial return because that is what investing is supposed to be. We can do something different with our assets. Let's open the barn doors and put that money to work for impact.

28. Blank and McGurn, *Is the Market Moral?*, 25.

# 5

## *All Investment Has Impact—What Is Ours?*

I use the term "impact investing" throughout this book because it is very commonly employed in describing the investment of capital for social impact and not just financial return. But it is a bit of a misnomer, as even impact investors will agree. For *all* investment has impact. All uses of capital influence lives and communities for good or ill, intentionally or unintentionally. Many of the "impacts" of the use of capital are not priced into the financial return.

Economists talk about "externalities" in markets. The cost of a good or service in economic models is the place where the demand for a product meets the supply of the product. The more people who want something and the less of it there is, the more it will cost. But this model takes into account only the value that a buyer is willing to pay a seller for the good or service. It does not include any other costs that occur in the larger system when that good or service is exchanged. There are often additional costs borne by people who are not involved at all in the initial transaction. They are called externalities. One externality is the environmental cost of oil extraction, which is not fully included in the price of oil. Another is the impact of air pollution that occurs when someone drives a car: this cost is not included in the purchase price of the car. The costs of these externalities are borne by the general public, vulnerable populations, the earth, and so on.

These externalities and other impacts are present wherever money is put to work. Even the term "externality" is not quite accurate because those impacts are not really external to the system. Rather they are part of the system. This is true in investing choices as well. While money itself may be neutral, the application of money in the world is never neutral. As Jed Emerson says, "capital is always at work, always in motion."[1] This reality should encourage us to be thoughtful and intentional about putting our money to work. Do we want our capital put to work by businesses seeking to create more needs among consumers that they can meet with the latest product, or could our capital be better put to work meeting the many pressing needs that already exist in our communities?

## Impact across the Life Cycle of Money

The way we interact with money matters. It is not neutral. This is true in all four parts of what I call the life cycle of money—earning, giving, spending, and saving.

We have talked a fair bit in the church about the theology around earning money—the theology of vocation. Are some jobs and ways of earning money less faithful to the way God has created us to live than others? Should we avoid jobs that exploit and damage others or the earth? Running a sweatshop and building weapons of war are some examples that provoke thought.

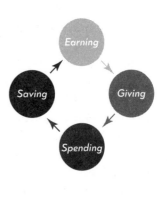

1. Jed Emerson, *The Purpose of Capital: Elements of Impact, Financial Flows, and Natural Being* (San Francisco: Blended Value, 2018), 224.

We've talked a lot about giving money away, about philanthropy. Stewardship is a very well-developed field in the church. There are many excellent books, seminars, conferences, and resources exploring the theology and practice of fund-raising and stewardship.

And more recently we've grown a lot in our thinking about spending money—after all, it was churches who started the fair-trade movement and raised awareness about how our buying choices influence lives around the world. It is common to find fair-trade coffee served in the fellowship halls of churches after worship.

But in many ways we've neglected the conversation about the impact of our saved money in the church. We will spend much time and effort ensuring that the $1,000 worth of coffee we buy each year for fellowship hour is fair trade, but we don't give much thought to what the $100,000 endowment we have invested in the stock market is doing. By and large, we are content to take high returns from whoever will give them to us without giving much thought to the impact of that capital in the world. If it is true that we put our money where our mouth is, it appears that right now we have more faith in Mark Zuckerberg than in our own people and communities. As Paul Sparks, Tim Soerens, and Dwight Friesen, founders of the Parish Collective, remind us: "Economics functions as a mirror where the truth about your faith is reflected back. The spreadsheet is a theological statement—where your treasure is, there your heart is also."[2] This is true in all four areas of the life cycle of money. It is vital that we give deeper consideration to the saving/investing phase.

Lynne Twist uses the metaphor of water when she explores "the soul of money."[3] Money, like water, flows through our lives, neighborhoods, and ecosystems. Sometimes it comes in a flood—there is lots

2. Paul Sparks, Tim Soerens, and Dwight Friesen, *The New Parish: How Neighborhood Churches Are Transforming Mission, Discipleship, and Community* (Downers Grove, IL: InterVarsity, 2014), 97.

3. Lynne Twist, *The Soul of Money: Transforming Your Relationship with Money and Life* (New York: Norton, 2017), 102–3.

of it—and sometimes in a trickle, when there is only a little. And like water, money can bring life and growth where it is allowed to flow. But if it is held back and dammed up, it gets stale and toxic. As in the parable of the rich fool, money produces nothing good for anyone when it is held onto too tightly.

The source of both money and water affects the health of what it does in the world. Brackish or polluted water from upstream will kill everything downstream. The same is true with money. The outflow of money is not only important; the source of that money is as well. If that source, how the money is earned, is not healthy, then its impact will not be good for the larger ecosystem even if the earnings are put to good use. The good that money may produce downstream can be undone, or even outdone, by the damage caused in making that money upstream. This is particularly true in how money makes money—in other words, in investing.

## Seeking Clean Upstream Sources of Money

In 2013 the archbishop of Canterbury, the senior bishop of the Church of England, rolled out an ambitious plan to put predatory payday lenders in the United Kingdom out of business. One of the worst offenders, Wonga, charged customers seeking short-term payday loans interest rates as high as 5,853 percent APR (annual percentage rate). (That comma is not a typo; Wonga was charging an interest rate of almost 6,000 percent.) Deeming this practice unethical, the church sought to support community financial institutions in order to encourage alternative lenders and with the goal of eventually putting Wonga out of business. But this worthy effort was undermined when it was revealed that the Church of England had invested some endowment funds in Wonga. So the church was making money off of the very same exploitative business it was trying to eradicate. Money the church was using for its mission downstream was polluted by the source upstream.

I encountered another powerful example of the impact of up-stream sources of revenue as an MBA student at the Wisconsin School of Business. I attended an evening lecture given by two prominent and very "successful" investment professionals who are graduates of the school. After listening to them speak for ninety minutes about how to succeed in traditional investing, I spoke with them for a few minutes at a post-lecture reception. I asked them what they thought of impact investing. Both men laughed. "Impact investing," they said, "just doesn't make sense." When I pressed them on why they thought that, they gave me a very classic two-pocket response, saying that rather than trying to do good with investment choices, savvy investors should seek to make as much money as possible from their money and then, if they choose to, give away some of the earnings to do good in the world.

They didn't use this analogy, but I imagine they would agree with venture capitalist Marc Andreesen, who said that impact investing is "like a houseboat. It's not a great house, and not a great boat."[4] In their view, making money should be entirely separate from supporting mission through philanthropy. Integrating the two, as impact investing does, is like the houseboat—not very good at either of its functions. I understand the critique but am not convinced. Perhaps impact investing is more like a smart phone—good at making calls *and* watching YouTube.

When I wouldn't just quietly walk away from the conversation, one of the speakers told me a story about how the California public pension fund system, which invests retirement savings for teachers and other public employees, decided a number of years ago to divest from tobacco companies. As a result, it lost an estimated $3 billion of value for the fund and therefore for its collective retirement savings. He expected me to be horrified by this "mistake" and quickly agree

---

4. Andreesen, quoted in Morgan Simon, *Real Impact: The New Economics of Social Change* (New York: Nation Books, 2017), 34.

that the teachers should never have left so much money on the table by not investing in tobacco. But the story confirmed for me the exact opposite. This investment "expert" was assuming that there was no value or impact in the upstream source of the teachers' earnings. The money they made or lost was neutral in his view. But this is not the case.

The farming and sale of tobacco have significant impact on the environment and society that is not captured in the financial return that tobacco companies would have provided the teachers' pension fund. As he told this story, I wondered, how much value did the teachers save society by not supporting the production of tobacco? Smoking-related illness in the United States costs us all more than $300 billion per year.[5] The World Health Organization reports that "The harmful impact of the tobacco industry in terms of deforestation, climate change, and the waste it produces is vast and growing," and tobacco kills more than seven million people per year.[6] California teachers may have viewed the cost of giving up $3 billion in their fund well worth the massive social savings brought about by a weakened tobacco industry. They understood that the source of their retirement income upstream mattered. Their investment choices were not neutral. Simply making as much money as possible, by whatever investment strategy is most lucrative, is not always the right choice.

A recognition of the importance of how money originates has led to the socially conscious screened-investing movement that has gained more traction than direct impact investing in the church.[7] Many endowments screen out "bad" companies from their investment portfolio—what are sometimes called "sin stocks." Tobacco,

5. Centers for Disease Control, "Economic Trends in Tobacco," last reviewed May 18, 2020, https://www.cdc.gov/tobacco/data_statistics/fact_sheets/economics/econ_facts/index.htm.

6. World Health Organization, *Tobacco and Its Environmental Impact: An Overview* (Geneva: World Health Organization; 2017), https://apps.who.int/iris/bit stream/handle/10665/255574/9789241512497-eng.pdf.

7. Often referred to as SRI (socially responsible investing) or ESG (environmental, social, governance screening).

weapons, gambling, and alcohol were eliminated early on. Some investors have moved to screening out fossil fuel companies, those that sell bulldozers that Israel uses to build walls in disputed territory, companies that treat workers poorly, and so on.

Often screened portfolios move heavily into so-called clean investments in technology—Amazon, Apple, Facebook, Google. But given what we are learning about the addictive qualities of Facebook, the environmental impact of the materials going into iPhones, and questionable behavior of Amazon in the marketplace, are these companies really clean? While it is vital to ask how "clean" an investment is, and screening our investments is essential, simply removing the worst companies from an investment portfolio still leaves most of our capital working to grow business and not making a positive impact in people's lives.

This is true even if we just put our money in the bank. The bank doesn't store it in a vault in the back. It immediately lends it out or invests it. Unless we literally put our money under a mattress, it is at work having an impact every single minute of every single day. Put another way: "Do you know where your money spends the night?" What impact is your capital having in the world right now?

# 6

## *Creating a New Future by*
## *Repairing the Past*

I f the purpose of capital is to make good in the world with what God has lent us, and the way we go about growing that capital makes a difference, how then are we to think about the role capital plays in perpetuating or eliminating injustice in our world?

### Lessons from the 1619 Project

Matthew Desmond helped shape my thinking about this in an essay he wrote as part of the *New York Times* 1619 Project. The 1619 Project is a look at the United States in 2019, four hundred years after people were stolen from their homeland in Africa and brought to the early colonies as slaves. The legacy of that sin remains deeply embedded in our society and is a major factor in the economic system and harsh inequality that we live with today. The 250 years of slavery and subsequent 100 years of Jim Crow citizenship forced upon Black people account for almost 90 percent of our nation's history. As Desmond writes, "historians have pointed persuasively to the gnatty fields of Georgia and Alabama, to the cotton houses and slave auction blocks, as the birthplace of America's low-road approach to capitalism."[1]

---

1. Matthew Desmond, "In Order to Understand the Brutality of American Capitalism, You Have to Start on the Plantation," *New York Times Magazine*, August 18,

According to Desmond, our culture of "acquiring wealth without work, growing at all costs, and abusing the powerless" is a direct descendant of slavery.[2] Slavery generated enormous wealth for many in the United States—wealth that remains at work in our society today. But that wealth was created on the backs of enslaved people; it was even embedded in their very bodies. At one point in our history, "the combined value of enslaved people exceeded that of all the railroads and factories in the nation."[3] In the mid-nineteenth century, "Slaves were the single largest, by far, financial asset of property in the entire American economy."[4] This value was driven up by the important role slaves played in harvesting one of the most valuable commodities of the time—cotton.

Wealth from cotton farming was made possible by two key inputs that were stolen by those who accrued all the wealth: land and people. Land was stolen from indigenous people, and people were stolen from their land. Together with financial markets and an endless appetite for more, enormous wealth was created for a select few and American capitalism was born. "Like today's titans of industry, planters understood that their profits climbed when they extracted maximum effort out of each worker."[5] This in turn led to horrific violence perpetrated against enslaved people, as planters sought to squeeze as much value and personal wealth out of their most valuable assets. As Desmond makes clear, "Unrestrained capitalism holds no monopoly on violence, but in making possible the pursuit of near limitless personal fortunes, often at someone else's expense, it does put a cash value on our moral commitments."[6]

---

2019, https://www.nytimes.com/interactive/2019/08/14/magazine/1619-america -slavery.html.

2. Desmond, "In Order to Understand," 40.

3. Desmond, "In Order to Understand," 32.

4. David W. Blight, quoted in Ta-Nehisi Coates, "The Case for Reparations," *Atlantic*, June 2014, https://www.theatlantic.com/magazine/archive/2014/06/the -case-for-reparations/361631/.

5. Desmond, "In Order to Understand," 34.

6. Desmond, "In Order to Understand," 36.

The economic model of extraction from many to create wealth for a few was not limited to the Southern white plantation. Northerners were also central to the development of this system by building textile mills to process the vast amount of cotton being produced and creating financial instruments that helped fuel the rapid expansion of land and people theft. Tiya Miles reminds us that "the original wall for which Wall Street is named was built by the enslaved at a site that served as the city's first organized slave auction."[7] Ta-Nehisi Coates describes the systematic and pervasive exploitation of African Americans trying to buy homes in Chicago—from redlining neighborhoods to exclude Black buyers to predatory lending that enriched whites and kept Black homeowners in a cycle of unending debt.[8]

One such financial instrument is the mortgage. Well before the mortgage (borrowing money to purchase a valuable asset) became synonymous with buying a house, mortgages were placed on enslaved people. "In colonial times, when land was not worth much and banks didn't exist, most lending was based on human property."[9] Thomas Jefferson mortgaged 150 enslaved workers to build Monticello. Mortgages on people were packaged and sold much like mortgages on homes are packaged and sold today. They became sophisticated financial instruments allowing investors to stay at arm's length from slavery even while making lots of money from its horrors. As time went on, and some grew uncomfortable with the idea of enslaving people for work, financial instruments remained a way for investors far from the cotton fields in geography and perceived values to get rich from slavery. Historian Calvin Schermerhorn asks a pointed question about the slave economy that rings just as true today: "We care about fellow members of humanity, but what do we do when we want returns on

7. Tiya Miles, "1619 Project: How Slavery Made Wall Street," *New York Times Magazine*, August 18, 2019, https://www.nytimes.com/interactive/2019/08/14/mag azine/slavery-capitalism.html.

8. Coates, "The Case for Reparations."

9. Desmond, "In Order to Understand," 37.

an investment that depends on their bound labor?"[10] We could insert "gentrification," "environmental degradation," "low wages," or any number of current sources of wealth extraction for "bound labor."

The legacy of slavery and stolen land is embedded in the very fabric of our economic system in the United States. Much of the wealth of our nation has roots in money made on the backs of enslaved people on land taken from Native Americans. And church institutions are just as bound up in this reality as are any other institutions. Pres House is built on the traditional, ancestral homelands of the Ho-Chunk, who lived in the Madison (Four Lakes) area long before Europeans arrived. Both Virginia Theological Seminary and Princeton Theological Seminary (my alma mater) have recently completed studies of their historic ties to slavery. Princeton Seminary currently has a $1 billion endowment. The source of this wealth is intimately tied to the enslavement of people. In the nineteenth century, donations to the seminary came from slaveholding individuals and congregations. For a period of time, the early seminary endowment was invested in Southern banks that were financing the expansion of slavery. As much as 30 to 40 percent of the seminary's pre–Civil War income can be traced to slavery. The first three professors of the seminary all used slave labor at some point in their lives—in some cases while teaching at the seminary. The upstream source of the seminary's current wealth is filthy and polluted.

## Is It Time for Reparations?

"So what?" some might ask. That was a long time ago. Institutions like Princeton Seminary reject slavery today and play an important role in educating new generations of church leadership who preach and lead efforts for justice. The money made from slavery genera-

10. Desmond, "In Order to Understand," 38.

tions ago is now being put to good use. Much of the income generated by Princeton Seminary's endowment today is used to provide
scholarships to help students complete their theological training and
serve the church in ministry. (For full disclosure, both my spouse and
I benefited from this money by receiving scholarships to attend the
seminary early in the first decade of the twenty-first century.) Isn't
the good that they are doing with the money enough to "clean" up
the sordid history of where that money came from?

Perhaps. Certainly putting "dirty" money to work for good in the
world is preferable to continuing to use it for harm. But is it enough?
Does the specific good that is done with tainted money matter? Is educating primarily white seminary students with money derived from
the slave trade an adequate "good" to repair the injustice of the past?
I am not convinced it is. Perhaps to more appropriately address the
injustices of the past, Princeton Seminary needs to put the proceeds
of that money to work in ways that more directly create a new form
of justice today. Perhaps reparations are in order.

Reparations is the idea of making amends for a wrong that has
been committed. Reparations is an attempt to restore justice and
often involves paying money to those who have been wronged. In
reviewing its history, Princeton Seminary took up the question of
making reparations for its legacy of benefiting from slavery. It framed
this in the theological language of repentance: "Our faith tradition
calls us to repentance after making confession. In making confession,
we tell the truth about our history before God and before the community of faith. In making repentance, we seek to make substantive
changes in our way of life as an act of contrition before God and those
we continue to hurt through the legacy of our community's sins."[11]
Princeton Seminary announced a number of action steps to address
the wrongs of the past, including funding scholarships for students

11. Princeton Theological Seminary, "Princeton Seminary and Slavery Report,"
accessed July 13, 2020, https://slavery.ptsem.edu/the-report/introduction/.

from historically disenfranchised communities, updating the curriculum, hiring a director for the Center for Black Church Studies, and hiring a new faculty member who will give attention to African American experience and church life. This will cost the seminary an estimated $1 million annually, and the seminary will reserve about $27 million of its $1 billion endowment to fund these changes.

While this is a good start, and I am grateful that my alma mater has named its complicity in benefiting from slavery, I agree with Nicholas Young, president of the Association of Black Seminarians, who has said this response, and the amount of money, is not enough.[12] To me, the steps outlined in the response are steps the seminary should be taking anyway—providing scholarships to underrepresented students, hiring good faculty, funding Black church studies. These are not a special kind of reparation but simply good practice for a seminary training pastors, educators, and social leaders. And setting aside less than 3 percent of its endowment for this purpose is inadequate. It feels like putting a Band-Aid on a person who needs an organ transplant. It is a small gesture toward healing and restoration but doesn't do much to reorder and rerepair the underlying injustice. As Coates bluntly states, "America was built on the preferential treatment of white people—395 years of it. Vaguely endorsing a cuddly, feel-good diversity does very little to redress this."[13]

What could the school do instead? What if Princeton Seminary set aside 10 percent of its endowment to invest in social enterprises started by its students when they graduate? Or invest that money in Black-owned businesses or social enterprises? What if Princeton Seminary divested some of its holdings in public securities or hedge funds and put that capital to work in the communities that are still dealing with the effects of slavery that enriched the seminary and left

12. Ed Shanahan, "$27 Million for Reparations over Slave Ties Pledged by Seminary," *New York Times*, October 21, 2019, https://www.nytimes.com/2019/10/21/nyregion/princeton-seminary-slavery-reparations.html.

13. Coates, "The Case for Reparations," 45.

many in our country way behind? Using some of the capital that has grown over the decades out of income from slavery to make deeper change might feel like more substantial restoration than spending money that the seminary should be spending anyway on things it should be paying for anyway. Investing significant portions of its large endowment in community development, job creation, housing, and wealth creation for those who have largely missed wealth growth would begin to move the needle toward justice. Edgar Villanueva, in his book *Decolonizing Wealth*, calls upon foundations throughout the country to voluntarily set aside 10 percent of their assets to create a fund from which Native Americans and African Americans could receive grants that would help create wealth and restore justice through funding for home ownership and start-up businesses.[14] Church institutions should lead the way. Impact investing, with church-owned assets, could contribute to restoration. They could create a new future by repairing the past.

As Pastor Sadell Bradley describes it, African Americans are struggling on a long and arduous journey from first being *owned* to now *owing* those who have taken advantage of racist lending practices, while they really seek and deserve *ownership*. The question facing our society now is whether African Americans will be given the opportunity to move into ownership so that the vast racial inequalities that exist between Black and white Americans will shrink rather than grow.[15] For this to happen, white individuals and historically white institutions must be willing to invest in Black-led businesses, neighborhoods, and social enterprises in such a way that ownership accrues to those who have for centuries created, but not benefited from, wealth. Done correctly, property and economic development using impact investing as fuel has the potential to shift wealth back

14. Edgar Villanueva, *Decolonizing Wealth* (Oakland, CA: Berrett-Koehler Publishers, 2018), 162.

15. From personal conversations with Melissa Sadell Bradley, pastor at the Warehouse Church, Cincinnati, OH.

from the descendants of slaveholders to the descendants of slaves. A renewed relationship with capital, as Villanueva powerfully argues, can serve as medicine to heal, restore, and decolonize wealth.[16] Such an approach begins to create a new future by addressing root injustice and repairing the past.

So, what role can the church play in all this? While we swim in the same waters and get wrapped up in the same lies of fear and greed as everyone else, the church has an opportunity to break free from these patterns and use our capital to seek justice rather than perpetuate it. As Rebecca Blank notes, a major point of "disconnection between Christianity and economic models of behavior is their assumption that more is better. Christianity affirms the value of abundance, but that abundance is measured not by the abundance of material goods but abundance of the Spirit."[17] Coates calls for "more than recompense for past injustices—more than a handout, a payoff, hush money, or a reluctant bribe. What I'm talking about is a national reckoning that would lead to spiritual renewal."[18]

We need a corrective. We need to recalibrate our relationship with money. We need to step back from the "way it has always been done" and think differently about how we use our capital.

16. Villanueva, *Decolonizing Wealth*, 7–9.

17. Rebecca Blank and William McGurn, *Is the Market Moral? A Dialogue on Religion, Economics, and Justice* (Washington, DC: Brookings Institution Press, 2004), 24.

18. Coates, "The Case for Reparations," 50.

# 7

## Reimagining Assets—
## a Higher and Better Use?

L et's return to the idea of redemptive entrepreneurship and impact investing. Of all the people and institutions that could be
leading the charge to rethink the use of capital, the church should
be on the front line. We may be behind the eight ball now, but faith
communities have led in the application of capital for good in the
past. It is time to reclaim this legacy.

### Reclaiming a Legacy

The origins of socially responsible and impact investing can be
traced back to 1758 when the Quaker annual meeting proclaimed that
members of the church could not profit from, and therefore invest in,
the slave trade.[1] New England Quakers required applicants for membership to compensate any former slaves they may have owned.[2] To
be a Quaker in late eighteenth-century New England meant paying
reparations. Quakers used their capital to address a deep, and literally
wicked, problem. It could be argued that the earliest Christian church
itself was the very first social enterprise, organized by Jesus follow-

1. Morgan Simon, *Real Impact: The New Economics of Social Change* (New York:
Nation Books, 2017), 32.
2. Ta-Nehisi Coates, "The Case for Reparations," *Atlantic,* June 2014, https://www
.theatlantic.com/magazine/archive/2014/06/the-case-for-reparations/361631/.

ers to serve the needs of widows, orphans, and others whom God especially cares about. The church is characterized by "the tension between the way the world is and the way the world could or should be," says Paul Bickley. And "it is this instinct that has led them to 'invent' again and again—the monastic tradition, schools, hospices and hospitals."[3]

In the mid-twelfth century, Rabbi Moses Maimonides laid out a scale describing the moral benefit of eight degrees of almsgiving. He described eight levels of givers in ascending order of superiority. The lowest level is those giving alms with a "frowning countenance." In the middle are variations of giving without being asked or without being known by the recipient as the giver. But the highest degree is reserved for those who do something akin to impact investing: they give the person in poverty a gift or a loan or a job to "strengthen his hand so that he would have no need to beg from other people."[4]

This ancient approach to addressing the "wicked" problems of our world seeks to not just address an immediate need in front of us but to go after the underlying causes of injustice and suffering. Richard Rohr challenges us when he writes that the church "organized itself around charity and almsgiving, but the church lost a deeper sense of solidarity, justice, simplicity, and a basic understanding of the poor . . . as good as charity is, it largely became an avoidance of basic concern for justice."[5]

God calls us to charity, almsgiving, and philanthropy. There will always be needs that require us to give money away, and it is clear throughout Scripture that God invites us to give freely and generously of all that we have. But charitable giving can mask the real work of justice making.

---

3. Paul Bickley, *Doing Good Better: The Case for Faith-Based Social Innovation* (London: Theos, 2017), 30.

4. As found in Jed Emerson, *The Purpose of Capital: Elements of Impact, Financial Flows, and Natural Being* (San Francisco: Blended Value, 2018), 302.

5. Quoted in Emerson, *The Purpose of Capital*, 223.

Charitable giving includes some risks and pitfalls, which the church has often fallen headlong into. One such hazard of giving money away is that the giver can quite easily end up in a position of power over the receiver, or at least feel some self-righteousness about being the one who can give to someone else who is in need. The way churches and churchgoers practice giving is often lacking in mutuality. There is little to no real relationship between the giver and the receiver. Money or goods are handed out from those who "have" to those who supposedly "have not." That does not empower the one receiving and does little to address the real injustice that created such inequality to begin with.

## A Lesson in Mutuality

I was fortunate enough to be taught something about this when I was a college student in Berkeley, California. During my sophomore year, my roommate and I started a service ministry to homeless neighbors out of People's Park. There were, and still are, many folks experiencing homelessness in Berkeley. Each Monday night we would cook some hot chocolate on a camp stove in the park (which we subsequently learned was illegal) and then walk along Telegraph Avenue sharing with anyone who wanted a warm drink. We'd get to know the names and stories of our neighbors who were living on the streets. The "program" was very simple—all we offered was a little something warm to drink, and the dignity of a real conversation, to people who were generally ignored by the student population.

One evening we had just finished cooking our hot chocolate and pouring it into thermoses to carry down the street. Just as we set off on our usual route, we ran into a small group of folks we had not met previously who were new to town. After sharing drinks and conversation for a while, we began to move on and make our way up the street. One of the women stopped me and pressed two one-dollar bills into my hand, saying, "Please take this. I love what you are doing out here and I want to help pay for the milk and hot chocolate for others." It was clear that the money was most of what she had on her, so I immediately said, "Oh no, we don't need this. You keep your money for whatever you need it for. We are fine." Her smile turned into an angry frown as she countered, "How dare you not take my money! Do you think you are better than me because I am homeless and you are not? I want to help. Take my money and don't be so proud."

I accepted her gift.

I never saw the woman again, but that conversation has stuck with me ever since. She was right. I was being proud. I was approaching the people I met on the street with a lack of mutuality, acting as if I had lots to offer them and they had nothing to offer me. It wasn't just her dollar bills that I was rejecting. I was rejecting relationship. I was rejecting mutuality. I was only willing to give and not willing to receive. I learned on the streets of Berkeley what the beloved television star Mr. Rogers understood perfectly: "It's so very hard, receiving. When you give something, you're in much greater control. But when you receive something, you're so vulnerable. I think the greatest gift you can ever give is an honest receiving of what a person has to offer."[6]

Social enterprise and impact investing offer an alternative approach to traditional charity in which giving is largely one way. Unlike unilateral charitable giving, impact investing expects a return on money that is invested and assumes the one receiving the investment has the capability to give something back. And social enterprise expects clients, customers, or recipients to pay something for the services rendered. These approaches transform one-way, unilateral charitable giving into something with more reciprocity, more mutuality.

6. Jeanne Marie Laskas, "The Mister Rogers No One Saw," *New York Times*, November 21, 2019, https://www.nytimes.com/2019/11/19/magazine/mr-rogers.html?fbclid=IwAR1M-HZvqdsDTHNp5iWOtt5HF8y-67RtFQ8VoEvwgGPstxkiPp2jzAkhBEw.

Mark Sampson says the concept of gift and reciprocity can perhaps be a guiding principle for engaging in faithful social enterprise. Sampson draws on the work of John Barclay when he suggests "to be human is to give and to receive."[7] For Barclay, "the one-way gift can be bad for the recipients of gifts not only because they may be psychologically humiliated or socially demeaned, but because they end up spiritually crippled. If we refuse to accept a return we are denying others the means by which they become rich in giving to us!"[8] For Barclay and Sampson, mutual giving is "a means of entering into the generosity and self-giving love of God."[9] Social enterprise and impact investing provide an alternative economic model that encourages mutuality, contributes to real justice, and helps us solve wicked problems in new ways.

Impact investment, while never fully replacing philanthropy, has the potential to be a vehicle for the church to reclaim solidarity and address the root causes of some of our most wicked problems. The faith-based investors surveyed by the Global Impact Investing Network who do engage in impact investing were most concerned about the following five focus areas: decent work and economic growth, affordable housing and clean energy, reduced inequalities, poverty, and good health and well-being. All are wicked problems.

Redemptive entrepreneurship is on the rise because people of faith care about the wicked problems facing our communities. College students and young adults at Pres House routinely tell us that the reason they stay involved in our community is because we preach about, discuss, and get involved in the real, raw issues that we face: climate change, income inequality, racial injustice, and the opioid epidemic, just to name a few. Young people in particular are not inter-

7. Mark Sampson, "The Promise of Social Enterprise: A Theological Exploration of Faithful Economic Practice" (PhD diss., King's College London, 2019), 165.

8. Sampson, "The Promise of Social Enterprise," 165.

9. Sampson, "The Promise of Social Enterprise," 165.

ested in a faith that is disconnected from the things that matter. They resonate with the words of the prophet Amos, who proclaimed,

> I hate, I despise your festivals,
>     and I take no delight in your solemn assemblies. . . .
> Take away from me the noise of your songs;
>     I will not listen to the melody of your harps.
> But let justice roll down like waters,
>     and righteousness like an ever-flowing stream.[10]

They want to be engaged in God's work in the world, solving the wicked problems of our day.

### Redemptive Entrepreneurship and Impact Investing

Young people also want to be active. Matt Overton, youth minister and founder of Mowtown Teen Lawn Care and the Columbia Future Forge, has built his youth ministry around programs that employ teenagers to do real work in their community. Much of traditional youth ministry has focused on passive activities where young people show up to be led in some games, listen to a talk, and sing some songs. While there is nothing wrong with any of these activities, Matt found that he was able to engage youth at a different level by employing them in a social enterprise. His social enterprise model of youth ministry meets practical needs for employment, provides real-world mentoring of youth, and is financially sustainable.[11]

And it isn't only young people who get excited about turning

---

10. Amos 5:21, 23–24.

11. Matt Overton, *Mentorship and Marketplace: A New Direction for Youth Ministry* (San Diego: Youth Cartel, 2019).

their faith commitments into a different sort of engagement in their communities through social enterprise. First Presbyterian Church, Atlanta, recently launched a new incubator for social entrepreneurs in the Atlanta area. The church raised money to provide significant start-up funding grants for individuals and enterprises who are seeking to affect their neighborhoods through redemptive entrepreneurship. They also invite members of the congregation to put their experience in their "day jobs" to work as mentors of the entrepreneurs the church partners with. The senior pastor has found this aspect of the experiment to be one of the most fruitful. There are members of the church who have not found deep fulfillment in attending worship services as a passive participant but whose faith has been enlivened and refreshed by serving alongside redemptive entrepreneurs working on addressing some of the deep problems facing their community.

Redemptive entrepreneurship and impact investing are not a magic solution that will work in all contexts or address all needs. But those tools can effect change quite differently than the traditional approaches we have taken to solving problems. "The days of our operating within a traditional, bifurcation of nonprofit versus for-profit, good versus evil, impact first versus finance first dualistic frame of the purpose of capital are surely dead and past, left behind us in a burial ground of other ideas once handy, now historic."[12]

Impact investing will never replace almsgiving or philanthropy. There will always be needs that we simply must meet. When Jesus instructs his disciples to give to those who ask, he never tells them to evaluate if the one asking is worthy of help. He is unconcerned about whether the giving "works." And he certainly doesn't look for a financial return on helping people. But some problems in our communities need different solutions than simply giving money away from one pocket that was made in the other pocket. There are places

12. Emerson, *The Purpose of Capital*, 105.

where our capital can be put to work for transformation much more powerfully than we might have thus far imagined. Impact investing need not replace philanthropy as a way to use money for good in the world. It expands the toolbox. As Paul Bickley notes, "Distributing the proceeds of socially responsible investment is a positive model, but the missional potential of impact investing for social value is enormous."[13]

It is clear that we are not broke. The church has huge pools of invested assets and is one of the largest landholders in the country. Countless buildings and church-owned properties will become available in the next decade for new purposes. Can we envision a higher and better use for all these assets? I hope so. Because, if so, we will engage people in addressing the most important problems of our day in a deep and transformative manner. We will encourage mutuality in our relationships. And we will create new financial models to fund this work.

13. Bickley, *Doing Good Better*, 58.

# 8

## *So Much Property!*

Consider a scenario from Madison, Wisconsin, where I live and work:

A few years ago our local presbytery had to close a church in the city. The lovely and faithful congregation had reached the end of its life, and it was time to celebrate the fruitful ministry of many decades and close the church. The building was sold to a local Muslim community, who have made it their home—a wonderful sharing of sacred space with our neighbors. The funds generated by the sale of the building (almost $1 million) were then given away to charities that members of the congregation cared about over the years. One of those charities was Pres House. We received a very helpful gift from the sale that we put to work in the lives of college students. Other charities in town also received generous gifts that helped them provide food, shelter, and other vital needs to members of the Madison community. The congregation left a beautiful gift for many.

But I have wondered since that time, what if we, the presbytery, had not given that $1 million away? As much as I was grateful as a nonprofit leader to receive some of the proceeds of the sale of the church, I wonder if we could have used those funds differently. What if we had used that money as seed funding for a permanent, revolving loan fund to help build affordable housing in the neighborhood around that church? Affordable housing is a very pressing need in Madison, as it is elsewhere in the country. It is particularly needed in the location where that church had operated. But funding to complete such projects is difficult to come by. Imagine what a powerful legacy that church, and our presbytery, could have left if we had invested that money in a housing project that would have provided affordable living space for people in Madison while generating a small financial return. The initial $1 million could have been used to help build a facility and then eventually the investment returned to the presbytery, with interest, to use again for more housing. The money would be at work over and over again, helping to transform our community.

## Addressing Root Problems

But even more important than retaining the initial capital, and earning interest on the investment, is the impact such a project could make in our community. Churches, and the charities that benefited from the gift upon the sale of the building, spend a lot of time, money, and energy working to meet the needs of people in our community who live in substandard housing. A lack of quality, affordable housing has a negative ripple effect throughout the community. When a child comes "home" from school to sleep in a car at night, as too many kids in Madison do, he or she is going to struggle to get homework done and succeed in school. Moving frequently creates stress for children and hampers educational achievement. "When families pay too much for housing, they have less money left over to spend on their other needs, including food, clothing, childcare and health care. If other income or housing options are unavailable, families are forced to make difficult tradeoffs among those basic necessities to meet housing expenses."[1] These are some of the problems churches and charities are

1. Joydeep Roy, Melissa Maynard, and Elaine Weiss, "The Hidden Costs of the Housing Crisis," Partnership for America's Economic Success, Pew Charitable Trust, 2008, https://www.pewtrusts.org/~/media/legacy/uploadedfiles/wwwpewtrusts

seeking to solve. Investing in affordable housing is one way to address root problems that cost a great deal in dollars and quality of life.

We cannot change what happened with the $1 million generated by the sale of that church in Madison. And I am sure the charities who received the money did important work with it. But that shouldn't stop us from reexamining how we could more effectively make change in our communities. Imagine a community where a collection of churches has an aggregate of $1 million of endowment money invested in traditional investments. The collective returns on that $1 million might average 5 percent annually. That amounts to $50,000 of investment earnings each year. Imagine that they gave all of it away to help address the negative outcomes caused by a lack of quality affordable housing in their community. That would be fantastic.

But now imagine if this same collection of churches came together to create a $1 million affordable housing fund from their endowments or investments. Such a fund could help close financing gaps and catalyze the building of affordable housing where it might not otherwise happen. Not a donation, this money would stay in service and be recycled over time, allowing for the creation of multiple housing projects. Rather than helping Facebook and Google grow their businesses, the money would be put to work helping house people in need of quality, affordable places to live. The churches would have an enormous social impact and earn some modest financial return on their investment. Now, instead of simply giving money away to help meet ongoing symptoms created by a lack of housing, these churches would be engaged in addressing the root causes of those needs by helping to provide a more permanent, long-term solution. Rather than just $50,000 per year buying some assistance, they have now put the whole $1 million to work solving problems.

---

org/reports/partnership_for_americas_economic_success/paeshousingreport finalipdf.pdf.

BUILD (Baltimoreans United in Leadership Development) was organized in the 1970s by clergy and lay leaders from Union Baptist Church, Heritage United Church of Christ, and St. Matthew's Catholic Church to focus on organizing around neighborhood issues such as police protection and improving housing. BUILD is affiliated with the Industrial Areas Foundation (IAF), an experienced community-organizing organization.

In 2008, organizers for BUILD gathered community members in two neighborhoods of East Baltimore to listen to neighbors and identify the greatest needs of the community. It became clear that the growing number of vacant and decaying properties was a serious concern in East Baltimore. In 2009, there were almost 650 vacant buildings and lots in the two neighborhoods. On some properties, trees were growing inside empty homes. In response to the expressed need of the community, BUILD began a major initiative to redevelop the neighborhoods from the strengths of each respective community.

Starting from near Penn Station in the Greenmount West neighborhood, and Johns Hopkins Hospital in the Oliver neighborhood, BUILD began buying up vacant properties and rebuilding homes with high-quality construction. As they developed homes and rental units, other developers entered the market. By 2017, vacant property had been reduced by 75 percent in Greenmount and by 89 percent in Oliver. As of spring 2018, 338 residential units had been completed and 104 were in the pipeline. A café was invited into the Oliver neighborhood, supported by below-market rent in one of BUILD's properties; a major new playground was added; and a troublesome liquor store was forced to leave and the building torn down. As I walked around the neighborhood in February 2018, I saw families and children walking past new homes that had once been vacant, on streets that had previously been mostly empty.

Much of BUILD's redevelopment was funded with a $10 million revolving equity fund that had been raised by offering $100,000 unsecured notes to churches, individuals, and foundations. Investors committed their capital for fifteen years and received up to 2 percent in interest payments each year. Those initial investors will soon receive their initial investments back in full.

Metro IAF, a partner of BUILD, is looking to replicate and scale their success with this project to continue building in Baltimore and other locations. They are raising capital for a $30 million fund that will function with similar terms as the original fund. IAF is putting in equity capital of its own and is seeking another $26 million in subordinated financing split into A and B class notes. Like the earlier funds, investors will receive their capital back in a balloon payment in ten or fifteen years (at the discretion of the fund) and will earn up to 2 percent per year in interest income.

Once the fund is in place, IAF expects to finance up to nine thousand units of affordable housing, 80 percent of which will be rental and 20 percent owner occupied. They will again build from strengths in communities in which they have a strong organizing presence, including Baltimore, Chicago, Durham, Milwaukee, Washington, DC, and other locations. Metro IAF welcomes additional investment from impact investors for this fund.

## Reimagining Buildings and Property

The sale of church property in my presbytery highlights another vital and valuable source of capital available to many churches and church institutions—buildings and property. While not all churches and institutions have investment funds, most churches own buildings and property. I agree with Patton Dodd, who recently wrote in the *Wash-*

*ington Post*, "I'm not about to propose that church real estate is a silver bullet in the affordable housing crisis. But it is absolutely the case that many churches are holding underutilized real estate—parking lots (and the airspace above them), vacant lots, and empty or mostly empty buildings."[2]

The potential impact from new uses of church property is enormous. The United Methodist Church in North Carolina owns property estimated to be worth $1.5 billion. They are the second- or third-largest landowner in the state. And that is just the property of one denomination. Imagine if we added the value and acreage of Presbyterians, Catholics, Baptists, and countless others. Methodist leaders in North Carolina have estimated that church property is in actual use about 12 percent of the week.[3] That is an abysmal utilization rate for an asset worth so much. And the future use of many of these properties is up in the air. The Western North Carolina Conference of the United Methodist Church estimates that almost a quarter of its congregations will close over the next five years, at a rate of from forty to fifty per year.[4] Multiply that number by all the conferences in the state, all the states in the country, and all the denominations facing similar closures, and the scale of church property going through transition comes into focus. The COVID-19 pandemic may speed up that time line.

Trinity Centres Foundation in Montreal has found a similar opportunity in Canada. Recent studies suggest that more than one-third

2. Patton Dodd, "Cities Need Housing. Churches have property. Can they work something out?," *Washington Post*, November 5, 2019, https://www.washingtonpost.com/religion/2019/11/05/cities-need-housing-churches-have-property-can-they-work-something-out/.

3. From Joel Gilland, president of Wesley Community Development Corporation, in a meeting about church assets in transition, April 27, 2020.

4. Yonat Shimron, "A North Carolina Nonprofit Helps Churches Convert Property from Liabilities into Assets," *Faith & Leadership*, February 4, 2020, https://faithandleadership.com/north-carolina-nonprofit-helps-churches-convert-property-liabilities-assets.

(ten thousand out of twenty-eight thousand) of the church buildings in Canada will close in the next ten years. But according to Graham Singh, the executive director of the foundation, church buildings are one of Canada's most underutilized asset class. "Traditional church worship and ministry models ceased to operate successfully some forty years ago and have not been replaced by anything new, particularly in the case of these historic buildings themselves. In other words, churches have resisted innovation to the point where the undercapitalization of their heritage buildings has reached an almost irreversible condition."[5] Trinity Centres Foundation is working to help churches regain their presence in communities, not only as spaces for sacred worship, but also as community centers and hubs of vital service activity.

Because of our track record at Pres House, I often receive phone calls from pastors, denominational leaders, and others asking how to redevelop their property. These conversations typically begin with questions about how to generate revenue from their property to offset declining funding from other sources such as congregational giving. Denominational bodies are also asking what to do with churches that are being closed and often sold.

Some examples include the following:

- A denominational judicatory is expecting to close numerous churches in the next five to ten years and doesn't know what to do with the property besides sell it. They don't have the capacity or expertise internally to look into, or carry out, alternatives such as property development, reinvestment of sale proceeds, etc. The churches closing are asking for their help, and they need assistance helping their congregations.
- A church near a university campus is looking at developing

5. Graham Singh, "Updating the Social Contract around Historic Places of Faith," *Municipal World*, May 2019, 5.

student housing on their A-plus property in order to serve the students on their campus and generate self-sustaining revenue. They need assistance thinking through the pros and cons of such a major project and need impartial, disinterested input in an environment where developers, banks, and other potential partners all have significant financial incentives at stake, thus making their partnership potentially more fraught.

- A church in a major US city purchased a very valuable property next to their already large physical plant and were about to commence development for rental income. But they stepped back from the project to more intentionally evaluate how their property and money could be better integrated with their mission to serve their community.

- A Christian college in a city has been facing flat or declining enrollment along with rising costs and is anxious about its business model. It has been looking at selling or redeveloping property to potentially address the financial concerns and an uncertain future but needs help in evaluating options and aligning the questions about money with its mission focus.

Money, mission, and property use are all facets of the same stone. Philip Krinks, CEO of the St. Martin's Partnership in the United Kingdom, an organization that helps social enterprises, businesses, charities, and public bodies grow and develop sustainably, believes that the intersection of property, mission, and investment is particularly fruitful for social enterprise. And for the church. He has found that one of the success factors for social enterprise is the aggregation of a physical asset, plus a revenue stream, plus some initial grant funding to get the revenue stream started. This is a model that the church has ample resources to replicate all over the place.

Projects are popping up from coast to coast using church property in new ways. Wesley Community Development Corporation (CDC) is helping some of those many congregations in North Carolina re-envision what can be done with those properties for both mission impact and financial sustainability. Wesley CDC has helped congregations start preschools and preschool and after-school programs, build affordable housing, lease their commercial kitchens, create coworking spaces, plant community gardens, open recreational facilities, and more.[6] Working groups of pastors and leaders in California have started developing affordable housing on church property under the moniker "YIGBY" (yes in God's backyard), a play on the acronym NIMBY (not in my backyard) that so often comes up when neighborhoods explore affordable housing.[7] Emory United Methodist Church in Washington, DC, completed a $55 million workforce and low-income housing facility in 2019 on their church property using a creative combination of government financing, low-income housing tax credits, and investment from the United Methodist Development Fund. Arlington Presbyterian Church, in Arlington, Virginia, won a Traditioned Innovation Award from Duke Divinity School in 2020 after selling their property, which enabled the construction of low-income apartment units and space for a bilingual training center. Exciting things are happening with church property in transition!

Another example of work that supports innovative uses of church buildings and property is through an organization I am helping to lead, RootedGood. RootedGood is a spin-off of an innovation lab called Matryoshka Haus that launched fifteen social enterprises and projects in London over ten years. Two cofounders and I relied on thirty-five years of collective experience in social innovation to create RootedGood, which empowers institutions, social enterprises, and entrepreneurs to solve wicked problems and make good in the world through engaging tools, training, and experiences. One of our core

6. Shimron, "A North Carolina Nonprofit Helps Churches Convert Property from Liabilities into Assets."

7. Alejandra Molina, "'Yes in God's Backyard' to Use Church Land for Affordable Housing," Religion News Service, November 12, 2019, https://religionnews .com/2019/11/12/yes-in-gods-backyard-to-use-church-land-for-affordable-housing/.

efforts, the Oikos Project, helps congregations to reimagine using their property to better serve their neighborhoods and to leverage their capital assets to promote social impact. By the end of the Oikos Project, each congregation will effectively design and launch a social enterprise that utilizes its church property in a new way.

Let me return to the church in Madison that distributed about $1 million from its sale. I suggested that we could have put that $1 million into a revolving loan fund to build affordable housing. But what if we had gone even a step further? What if we had used that money to help build affordable housing on another church property? What if one church provided the property and others provided the investment? In that instance, all three elements could have come together: mission, money, and property. Mission: meeting a vital community need for affordable housing and transforming lives and neighborhoods. Money: putting money to work as an impact investment in a revenue-generating social enterprise. Property: providing the land on which to build that social enterprise. I can imagine numerous areas of the country where a model like this could work. Some churches could be sold to generate investment funds for other churches to launch social enterprises on their property. In this way the capital assets multiply upon each other for greater impact.

There is a lot of underutilized and soon-to-be-sold property out there. There will be grief and sadness as so many churches close in the coming years. Of this there is no doubt. Just as when a loved one dies, we must allow ourselves the space to celebrate past joys and mourn our losses.

At the same time there is also an incredible opportunity to reimagine how church property could be used for innovation and transformation during this unprecedented time of assets in transition. For even as the changes and closures come fast and furiously, we aren't broke. Death, and resurrection, is central to the Christian faith. Just as the cycle of death and life turns fallen leaves into spring flowers, the closure of churches provides space and fertilizer for new growth to spring up. The closing and selling of churches will free up millions of dollars of "new" money and unused property in the next decade. Shifting the primary use of a church property from Sunday services to coworking space that creates community is not failure—it is transformation. Supplementing income and mission activity by turning an unused education wing of a church into a grocery co-op that addresses a neighborhood food desert is not failure—it is innovation. Closing a congregation after many years of fruitful ministry, tearing down the church building, and repurposing the property for affordable housing is not failure—it is rebirth. We may grieve the changes. We should celebrate the past. But let us also look forward to new life and what God will do through us next.

# 9

## Barriers That Hold Us Back

M any of the ideas I have written about thus far are not unfamiliar in the church. Churches often speak about justice. Readers of the Bible know that Jesus talks about money more than just about any other subject. Church board meetings are full of conversations about budgets and stewardship and property use. So, why, as I noted in chapter 2, is so little impact investing and social enterprise being done in the church? Why do we persist with a two-pocket model when it comes to our money? And why do we use the language of scarcity so frequently when billions of dollars of church money are flowing through our economy every second of every day? What are some of the barriers that make it so difficult for us to actually do things differently? What is holding us back?

In this chapter I will explore some of the barriers that make it difficult for us to move from theory to practice and to implement new economic models in the church. By understanding the barriers, we can move past them to imagine, and create, something new.

### Lack of Access to Impact Investment Options

The Global Impact Investing Network (GIIN) launched a project in 2019 to study the state of faith-based impact investing globally. They observed that faith-based investors from around the world hold large sums of invested assets and share values that align with impact investing. But faith-based impact investing is not happening on as wide a scale as might be expected given this values alignment.[1] As noted earlier, impact investing represents only 11 percent of total assets under management.[2] So the GIIN set about to better understand faith-based impact investing through a major survey, one-on-one interviews, and meetings with faith-based investors. The GIIN study confirmed that while faith-based investors have a robust track record with shareholder activism and divestment movements, they have been quite slow to engage in impact investing. They highlighted a few barriers that hinder impact investing among faith-based institutions. One major barrier is a lack of access to impact investment options.

Many faith-based organizations are smaller institutions that have trouble accessing impact investment at a practical level. Some of the most interesting and impactful investment options are private debt and private equity investments (together, those private placement investment classes represent 48 percent of impact investments faith-based investors make). These types of investments can be harder to find, evaluate, and access than publicly traded securities. Smaller faith-based institutions may not have the capacity or knowledge either to underwrite private debt arrangements or to evaluate private equity investments.

There may also be a mismatch in investment size between investor and recipient. In some cases, minimum investment sizes for private placement investments are significantly larger than publicly traded investment options, and this prevents smaller faith-based institutions from investing in such ventures. On the flip side, small social enterprises are often looking for relatively modest investments, which are too small for large faith-based institutions that have minimum invest-

1. Global Impact Investing Network, "Faith Based Impact Investing: Growing the Field; Global Impact Investing Network Webinar," Global Impact Investing Network, December 18, 2019, https://www.youtube.com/watch?v=yvofIxMQqMk &feature=youtu.be.

2. Among faith-based investors who responded to the GIIN study.

ment purchase sizes. For example, a large endowment may be looking to place money in multimillion-dollar increments, while redemptive entrepreneurs on the ground are looking for six-figure investments. These mismatches are like putting a round peg in a square hole, and so deals simply don't happen.

This lack of access and inability to match investment size are real barriers. However, there are more and more options in the investment space that make accessing impact investments more feasible for smaller organizations. Working Capital for Community Needs (WCCN), for example, takes investments as small as $500 from individuals and institutions.[3] One does not need to be a high-net-worth investor to invest in WCCN. Investment advisers, when pressed, can usually provide access to some impact investment options for just about any size investor. If yours cannot, it may be time to find a new adviser. Finally, there are new impact investment funds being envisioned and proposed that are specifically designed to service faith-based investors and help solve issues of access. These types of funds are a growth opportunity.

### Lack of Access to Capital for Redemptive Entrepreneurship

If the first barrier is a problem for investors looking to put capital to work differently, the second barrier is a problem on the other side of the coin. In this current moment at least, many redemptive entrepreneurs with exciting and deeply meaningful enterprise ideas do not have access to capital. The number one theme in Echoing Green's 2020 study of the state of entrepreneurship was a lack of capital for frontline communities.[4] This may seem like an odd problem—if there

---

3. See p. 147.
4. Echoing Green, "State of Social Entrepreneurship 2020," Echoing Green, March 30, 2020, https://echoinggreen.org/news/state-of-social-entrepreneurship-2020/.

is money looking to be placed and people looking for money, surely they should be able to connect! But often the structural barriers described here get in the way. And at other times the connections between entrepreneurs and investors are simply not there.[5]

One of the most common sources of start-up capital for new entrepreneurs is what is called "friends and family money." Friends and family are asked to be the first investors in many new businesses and ventures. But what do entrepreneurs do when their friends and family don't have money to invest, as is the case in many low-income/low-wealth communities? A friends-and-family approach to entrepreneurship preferences the wealthy with wealthy connections who can put money into the very early, risky start-up phase of a new venture. As Simon observes, "Entrepreneurship is a birthright for some, and an incredible struggle for others."[6] Mitch and Freada Kapor note, "genius is evenly distributed by zip code; opportunity is not."[7] Church networks can function like a friends-and-family network for those who don't have family or friends with money. We often speak of the church as the family of God. But we have to be intentional about this.

There are billions of dollars of capital in the church. But most of it is held by predominantly white-led institutions like the Presbyterian, Episcopal, and other mainline churches. African American churches and immigrant churches have far fewer resources and assets to work with, even though they do some of the most innovative work on the ground. For example, only 5 percent of Black Protestant congregations have an endowment, while 59 percent of mainline Protestant congregations have one.[8] Similarly, well-established church institu-

5. I describe an example of this in chapter 11 with my friend Nikki Hoskins and her tiny-homes enterprise that has struggled to find capital investment.

6. Morgan Simon, *Real Impact: The New Economics of Social Change* (New York: Nation Books, 2017), 59.

7. Quoted in Simon, *Real Impact*, 59.

8. Lake Institute on Faith and Giving, "The National Study of Congregations' Economic Practices," Indiana University Lilly Family School of Philanthropy, 2019,

tions have far more resources than newer ones. Sixty-three percent of congregations founded before 1900 have an endowment, while only 2 percent of those founded in the last ten years have one.[9]

As we dismantle some of our barns storing excess capital and release it into the world, it is vital that those funds don't end up simply moving from one privileged owner to another. We do not want to replicate the way investment is done in the wider venture capital world, where less than 1 percent of venture capital investments are made in businesses founded by African Americans.[10] And even though 38 percent of new businesses in the United States are started by women, less than 6 percent of those founders receive venture capital funding.[11] Brandon Anderson, an entrepreneur and Echoing Green fellow, explains, "The reason you see Black people struggling to raise money, build a company, or start a movement, is not because they aren't good at it. It's certainly not because they aren't as capable as people who have the resources. It's because of the way this all started out. The U.S. was founded on and continues to operate with the exploitation of Black labor. If you understand that, you'll come to the work more humble as a funder."[12]

Morgan Simon sounds a further word of caution: "If the ownership of social enterprises remains limited to the privileged, then it is difficult to imagine how impact investments can ultimately maximize benefit to communities, or facilitate any sort of significant resource

https://www.nscep.org/wp-content/uploads/2019/09/Lake_NSCEP_09162019-F-LR.pdf.

9. Lake Institute, "The National Study of Congregations' Economic Practices."

10. Daniel Applewhite, "Founders and Venture Capital: Racism Is Costing Us Billions," *Forbes*, February 15, 2018, https://www.forbes.com/sites/forbesnonprofitcouncil/2018/02/15/founders-and-venture-capital-racism-is-costing-us-billions/#3390ef4b2e4a.

11. "Why VCs Aren't Funding Women-led Startups," Wharton School of Business, May 24, 2016, https://knowledge.wharton.upenn.edu/article/vcs-arent-funding-women-led-startups/.

12. Echoing Green, "State of Social Entrepreneurship 2020."

transfer from the Global North to the Global South (or generally within any nation, from rich to poor)."[13] Investors need to intentionally seek to place capital in social enterprises, businesses, and nonprofits owned by people of color and others who exist in more marginal spaces, and to ensure that ownership and leadership are primarily vested in those communities.

### Lack of Knowledge, Expertise, and Awareness

Some faith-based institutions lack adequate knowledge about impact investing. And many redemptive entrepreneurs lack the appropriate training and expertise to be successful in launching sustainable social enterprises.

On the investment side, fund managers surveyed by the GIIN reported that one of the biggest barriers to securing faith-based investment in impact funds is that the "investor lacks knowledge or familiarity with impact investing."[14] This lack of knowledge takes two general forms: (1) a lack of technical knowledge and (2) a lack of awareness about what is possible and available. The former is more common for smaller organizations that do not have professional investment staff and, therefore, the technical expertise to access impact investments or build portfolios that include anything beyond very standard investment products. The latter is a barrier for religious investors of all sizes.

Many investors rely on outside advisers or wealth management teams at banks to provide investment advice, build portfolios, and conduct transactions. Often such advisers do not routinely offer impact investment options to their clients, and so investors end up

13. Simon, *Real Impact*, 49.
14. Global Impact Investing Network, "2019 Annual Impact Investor Survey," https://thegiin.org/assets/GIIN_2019%20Annual%20Impact%20Investor%20Survey_webfile.pdf.

investing in whatever these advisers suggest. For some advisers, building impact investment options into their clients' portfolios is more costly or complicated, so they avoid such investments. Others are simply not aware of the options or misunderstand the risk-and-return profiles, so they steer investors away or don't even bring up such options with them.

Sometimes volunteer or clergy leaders in congregations and other religious institutions do not really understand how investment works or don't believe they should be involved in detailed decisions about money since they are supposed to be focused on "ministry." These leaders may be even more likely to trust financial advisers without asking questions about where their money is spending the night, or if there are other ways to put their capital to work in the world. There are two kinds of institutions that are least likely to make changes in their investment approach. One kind lacks technical knowledge (or believes they should stay out of that kind of business). These are often smaller and less-resourced organizations. The other kind runs sophisticated investment operations believing they know how it should be done and are not open to exploring alternatives. These are often large and wealthy institutions that have technical knowledge but lack imagination for diverse ways of putting their significant investment capital to work differently.

Individuals and church-related institutions interested in engaging in redemptive entrepreneurship are also often lacking the knowledge, expertise, and training required to be successful in launching social enterprises. Seminary training still largely assumes a classic model of the preaching pastor whose primary form of ministry is Sunday worship services and pastoral care. Denominational leaders are typically drawn from the ranks of clergy and come into their work with similar training.

The good news is, this lack of awareness and knowledge is easily corrected. Even though investing isn't taught at seminaries, and investment professionals seem to speak a different language, most of what happens in investing is not overly complicated or beyond under-standing. Yes, the terminology and tools of investing might seem like Greek to some, but plenty of seminary students have learned Greek and managed just fine. Investing, and impact investing in particular, can be learned.

And likewise, social entrepreneurship can be taught. Numerous excellent accelerator programs are available for individuals and orga-nizations interested in experimenting in redemptive entrepreneur-ship, including the Make Good program created by RootedGood, Do Good X run by the Forum for Theological Exploration, and pro-grams by Praxis Labs. Attending SOCAP, the world's largest impact-investing conference, is a good way to learn more about impact invest-ing from a myriad of angles. A new gathering of faith-based investors and entrepreneurs called Faith and Finance is also worth considering. Launched in 2020 by the same folks who founded SOCAP, it has a more explicit faith-based lens. And of course, reach out to me. I am happy to point people toward further resources to build knowledge and awareness.[15]

## Satisfaction with Doing Good through Operations Rather Than Investment

This is two-pocket thinking at work—that money is made through investment and revenue on one side and then given away for good on the other side. Some faith-based investors fully subscribe to Bill Gates's two-pocket approach to money. In fact, almost half of the faith-based investors surveyed by the GIIN said they were satisfied with doing good in the world through operations rather than through

15. If you are interested in going beyond what I have written about in this book, I encourage you to see the bibliography for further reading.

investment.[16] The study found that large organizations tend to see programmatic activity as their primary objective and are therefore hesitant to invest in unfamiliar, riskier, or lower-return strategies that might reduce investment income.[17] They prefer to earn returns on invested assets that can then be put to work for program and operations. This may take the form of a willingness to invest in everything and anything for financial return in order to focus on doing good through operations. Or an organization may be satisfied with negatively screening out "bad" companies from their portfolio but is unwilling to consider a more active, positive, impact investment choice. More than 50 percent of religious investors are satisfied with the negatively screened investment options they have and therefore do not engage in active impact investing.[18]

I understand this position. As the director of a nonprofit that relies in part on income from invested assets for our operations, I understand that the focus of our mission is on what we do, not on how our money is put to work through investment. That order of priority is appropriate. After all, most faith-based investors are not primarily in the investment business—they are in the mission business. Thus program and operations take top priority in terms of time, attention, and resources. In many cases, there isn't even any bandwidth to consider investment decisions in detail. I have said to investment advisers, "Please find the best way to get the highest return with the lowest risk for us in the coming year, because we need the income to serve our students."

But as I have explained, this two-pocket approach is a fallacy. Even if we want to, it is impossible to separate money from mission. And beyond that reality, we can do even *more* good in the world if we consider not just our program and operations but *also* how our invested

16. Global Impact Investing Network, "2019 Annual Impact Investor Survey," 47.
17. Global Impact Investing Network, "Faith Based Impact Investing."
18. Global Impact Investing Network, "2019 Annual Impact Investor Survey," 47.

capital is put to work. I hope readers will be challenged to think about their invested money at work in the world. It can do more good than we first imagine.

## Felt Need for "Market-Rate" Returns, Risk Profile, and Liquidity

One of the greatest barriers to moving more church capital into social enterprise and impact investing is our obsession with market-rate returns, low risk, and high liquidity (the ability to quickly convert an investment to cash). The GIIN study confirms this reality. They found that more than three-quarters of investors are reluctant to engage in impact investing because they are concerned either that target returns will be not be achieved or about exit options and liquidity. In other words, they are afraid impact investments will not make enough money.

In fact, a full two-thirds of faith-based investors that do impact investing are still seeking market-rate returns in their impact investments. While some impact investments can earn market rate or above, not all investments can generate performance that matches the returns of Exxon Mobil or Facebook. Many investment committees, policies, and professionals aim to reach very specific, and quite aggressive, financial return numbers each year. This is often driven by the mission of the organization—as noted above, they need those returns in order to fund the mission as the financial model has been designed.

Pension funds are one such example. Pension funds have a very important, and very rigorous, fiduciary responsibility: to manage their funds in such a way that pensions can be paid out to those in retirement. This is a serious and vital task. Many pension funds do not feel that they can take lower returns than what is available in the market when pensions are on the line. The Employee Retirement Income Security Act of 1974 and subsequent guidance from the Department of Labor and the IRS direct pension funds to "act in the interest of the participants and their beneficiaries; and act for the exclusive purpose of providing benefits to workers participating in the plan and their beneficiaries."[19] As the GIIN found, pension funds thus typically look for safe, predictable, market-rate returns in order to meet fiduciary duties.[20] Sylvia Poniecki at Wespath Benefits and Investments, which manages retirement funds for the United Methodist Church, explains, "As a fiduciary, we need to make sure that we are well protected long term and that our participants are made whole in the event of a loss."[21]

This fiduciary duty guidance has typically been understood to mean that a fiduciary cannot take lower than "market-rate" returns on investments. At first glance, therefore, it would appear that pension funds cannot engage in impact investing if such investments do not match the risk-adjusted return of standard benchmarks. There is a lot of discussion, however, about the merits of this long-held assumption. We must ask if measuring performance of an investment against short-term benchmarks is really the right measurement in a world where climate change and income inequality create long-term risk that is not fully priced into the returns of a standard benchmark.

For example, oil and gas company investments often perform well when compared with short-term benchmarks. Extracting and selling raw material for energy creation from the earth can be quite lucrative. Investing in oil and gas companies that pay back an above-market return might appear to be a good way to exercise fiduciary responsibility and act in the interest of plan participants. Oil and gas consumption puts the future of our planet at risk, however, and thus creates long-term risk for plan participants' future financial and

19. Internal Revenue Service, "Retirement Plan Fiduciary Responsibilities," last updated December 20, 2019, https://www.irs.gov/retirement-plans/retirement-plan -fiduciary-responsibilities.

20. Global Impact Investing Network, "Faith Based Impact Investing."

21. Quoted in Amit Bouri, "GIIN: Why Impact Investing Is a Natural Fit for Faith-Based Investors," *Financial Advisor*, August 12, 2019, https://www.fa-mag .com/news/faith-in-finance--why-impact-investing-is-a-natural-fit-for-faith-based -investors-51034.html; and in personal conversations.

general well-being. So we must ask ourselves: Is measuring financial return on short-term metrics while ignoring long-term risks really acting in the best interest of plan participants? Perhaps the better long-term approach to fiduciary responsibility is to engage in careful and intentional impact investment that takes a longer, deeper, and wider view of investment "return." It may be that some impact investments are too risky or require too much of a concessionary return to meet a reasonable interpretation of fiduciary duty. But there are many impact investments that pension funds and other fiduciary agents could reasonably make. And some are.

Impact investing among pension funds, although limited, is taking place. And almost half of fund managers surveyed by the GIIN said they believe this type of investing will grow in the future.[22] I believe this will come about as a result of participants of pension funds asking for it. Tim Macready, CIO of the Australian superannuation fund Christian Super, explained that his organization's involvement in impact investing was prompted by beneficiaries: "Our members and beneficiaries asked us what good we were doing with their retirement savings, and how we were investing those savings for their future."[23]

I resonate with this personally. The money that is invested in my own pension plan by the Presbyterian Church is not someone else's money. It is my money. And the money of everyone in the plan. If together we decide that we want our invested money to do something different in the world, then our pension plans will have to respond to those requests. If we tell our fund managers that acting in our best interest includes factoring in the social impact of the investments, then investment decisions will change.

22. Global Impact Investing Network, "2019 Annual Impact Investor Survey," 47.

23. Quoted in Bouri, "Why Impact Investing Is a Natural Fit for Faith-Based Investors."

## Narrow View of Acceptable Partners and Theological Litmus Tests

One of the barriers to more faith-based impact investment and social enterprise that worries me the most is the tribalism of the Christian church and a tendency to fixate on narrow theological litmus tests for whom we will work with. I am afraid we will trip over ourselves in the process of trying to put capital to work for good.

Attaching the term "Christian" or "faith-based" to anything creates problems immediately. What do those terms mean? There is no universally understood definition of what Christian investing or faith-based social enterprise means. Does Christian investing mean investing money in ventures that spread the Christian faith? In ventures run by Christians? In ventures that further "Christian values"? And what even are "Christian values"? If an investor is putting money into my social enterprise, do we have to agree on our theology? What parts of our theology? This is particularly fraught in a moment in our society where people are so divided across cultural and political lines.

Let's pick a particularly thorny current issue as an example. The ministry I lead at Pres House is fully welcoming and affirming of LGBTQ+ individuals. We believe God calls us to welcome all of God's children and recognize that God has created us all as good, no matter what our sexual orientation or gender identification. Many of our leaders and staff identify as LGBTQ+. Our church community is often the first place where LGBTQ+ young adults have ever been invited to follow and worship Jesus while being fully accepted for who they are. Finding such a space is utterly transformative for their faith and life. When we say, "You belong," we really mean everyone who walks through our doors.

Some Christian investors will not invest in our social enterprise because they do not share our understanding of Christian values. They do not want to invest in a project that affirms "the gay lifestyle."

In the same way, I would not be inclined to invest in a Christian organization that promotes gay conversion therapy or discriminates on the basis of sexual orientation or gender identification. I do not want to use my money to support an organization that is hurtful toward my LGBTQ+ siblings and friends. A similar scenario could play out for any number of hot-button issues or theological litmus tests.

This narrow view of what is acceptable or not for faith-based investing might also play out along denominational lines. Will Presbyterians be willing to invest in Methodist enterprises? Will Catholic institutions be willing to invest in Lutheran projects? Or will we stay locked in our silos? Once we go down the faith-based investment road, will we become mired in a sort of sacred/secular quagmire where only "Christian" projects are suitable investments? What if the best project in our neighborhood doing the most good for our community is run by someone of another faith tradition entirely? How broadly do we define redemptive entrepreneurship? Can a Muslim engage in redemptive entrepreneurship? (For the record, I personally believe the answer to that is yes.)

I've seen this sort of challenge play out in other analogous applications. When online donor giving was in its early stages, I was often asked by other church leaders and campus ministers what platform to use for online giving on their websites. They focused on platforms created by the Presbyterian Foundation or other "Christian" providers. Those products are fine. But so are PayPal, Stripe, and other "secular" tools that often work better with lower fees. But because they didn't have a denominational or Christian label attached to them, church entities didn't trust them.

The ironic thing about all this is that most investors, including Christians, do not approach their general investing with this sort of precision. Most Christian investors do not evaluate Facebook or Google on their LGBTQ+ inclusion policies, or ask what Jeff Bezos believes about abortion before they invest in Amazon. We are happy to accept the financial returns and remain "agnostic" on the values of those founders. But as soon as we start talking about "faith-based" investing, these questions about theology come up immediately. Perhaps this is because, like a family at Thanksgiving, we are most likely to have conflict within our own families over the issues that matter to us.

I don't have a simple solution to this particular problem. And I don't raise this to suggest that it isn't important or that we should just set aside our values when it comes to faith-based investing. That is inconsistent with my entire message in this book. It is vital that investors and redemptive entrepreneurs develop clarity around values that are important to each of us when engaging in this work.

I raise this concern because I believe it could be a major stumbling block in the growth of this movement and the potential to make powerful change in the world. I hope we won't get so tripped up by theological disagreements and litmus tests that we don't engage in the really important work that needs to happen in our neighborhoods and communities. There is simply too much at stake to refuse to work together across denominational, theological, and interreligious boundaries.

While it is easy in the church to separate ourselves into ever thinner and thinner slices of "correct" theology, the fact is, when facing the wicked problems of our world, we are all in this together. Does partnering and investing for social good mean that we have to agree 100 percent of the time on 100 percent of the issues? I hope not, for if that were true, we would never do anything. None of us is totally "pure" in the way we put our money to work and its alignment with our values and convictions. We do the best we can in the midst of complexity, weighing a myriad of considerations as we make decisions. And we are called to reach across aisles, differences, and distances of all kinds in order to love the "other" and work together for the common good. Jesus went out of his way to eat with the unclean, told stories like the Good Samaritan to highlight the breaking down of divisions, and reconciled all to God and each other.

We would do well to keep that in mind as we work and invest.

* * *

The barriers I have been describing are real, but they are not insurmountable. And it is worth our effort to overcome them in order to put more money to work for good in our world. So let us not be satisfied with the way things have been done before or with the way we have been told things should be done. Our assumptions are a construct of our own making. Let us seek to do more good with the capital that God has lent us for the time we have.

In part 2 of this book, I describe some of the ways we can engage in this work effectively while negotiating the barriers I've named above. I offer some ingredients to make it work for redemptive entrepreneurs and investors who want to give it a try, open the barn doors, and put the assets we do have to work for mission impact and financial resiliency.

# PART TWO

# Ingredients to Make It Work

Perhaps by now you are convinced that this idea of investing church capital differently and experimenting with social enterprise is worth trying or at least exploring further. Perhaps you are concerned that businesses are using church money to expand their operations in ways that are inconsistent with your values. Or you agree that we could do more with all the money and property God has lent us for such a time as this, rather than settling for the 5 percent earnings we receive from our portfolio or the 12 percent actual usage time of our buildings. Perhaps the idea of addressing deep injustices by shifting ownership or solving the root causes of wicked problems is compelling. It could be that a vision for earning sustainable revenue while also reengaging people in the work of the church is exciting. Perhaps for all of these reasons you are interested in giving this a try.

How then do we do it? How do we do it well? How do we engage in impact investing and social enterprise that is faithful to the Christian tradition, respectful of our communities, and effective in outcomes? Even if we do overcome some of the barriers from chapter 9, there remain perils and risks in engaging in this work. Living faithfully with what God has given us is not an easy, straightforward task. It is a journey that requires discernment, reflection, learning, and practice. Jumping into impact investing or social enterprise because it is new and "sexy" without eyes wide open is foolish. As much as I believe in the power of redemptive entrepreneurship and impact investment, these tools and approaches are not perfect or without their own perils. Many variables and ingredients go into a fruitful faith-based impact investing relationship.

In the next two chapters I will suggest five key ingredients that will help redemptive entrepreneurs and investors succeed. These ingredients are described from both sides of the investor/enterprise relationship, and they complement each other. The core belief underlying all these principles is the hope and promise of abundance—that we have something in our communities, churches, and institutions, and that we can put it to work for great things. As Rev. George Harrison wrote in 1964, "The reason we have accomplished so little for God and [the] church is that we have conditioned ourselves to think small and to expect small. We have been extremely successful in attaining our small goals."[1] Let us dream big, not small. And let us use what God has entrusted to us to take risks, be creative, and transform lives.

||||||||||||||||||||||||||||||||||||||||||||||||||||||||||||||||||||||||||||||||||||||||||||||||||||||||||||||||||||||||||||||||||||||||||

1. James Hudnut-Beumler, *In Pursuit of the Almighty's Dollar: A History of Money and American Protestantism* (Chapel Hill: University of North Carolina Press, 2007), 175.

# 10

## *Ingredients to Make It Work for Redemptive Entrepreneurs and Social Enterprises*

I love riding bicycles. Ever since I was a little boy, I've loved the freedom, speed, and feeling of working hard a bicycle offers. I am an amateur bike racer, and I consider it a good year when I put more miles on my bike than on my car. I love watching bike racing, a sport many consider more boring to watch than golf (it isn't, really!). My daughters don't know anything about football or baseball, but they know all the top riders in the Tour de France each year because that is what is on our TV.[1]

Your eyes are the two most important parts of your body when riding a bike. Yes, your legs turn the pedals, and your heart pumps the blood. But your eyes direct where the bike is going to go. When you watch people learning to ride a bike, you often see them look down at their pedals or at the front wheel. I know from experience that does not work well. If you are looking down, you will wobble all over the road. To ride forward, you must look forward. In fact, you need to keep looking at the place you want to go. If you look at the curb while riding, you will almost certainly hit the curb. If you look directly at the pothole you want to avoid, there is a good chance you will fall right

---

1. Some of this is adapted from a blog post I wrote for Princeton Seminary: "Look Ahead to Where You Want to Go," *The Thread* (blog), Princeton Theological Seminary, accessed July 20, 2020, https://thethread.ptsem.edu/leadership/look-ahead -to-where-you-want-to-go.

into it. But if you look up the road at the part of the pavement that is clear, that is where you will go. You will go where you are looking.

## Focus on the Core Mission

The same principle applies when moving into redemptive entrepreneurship and social enterprise. The first and most important step to getting somewhere new is to fix your attention on where you want to be. Not on where you are now, not on the obstacles in the path; you must fix your attention on where you want to be. You will go where you are looking. Staying focused on core mission is a lot like riding a bike.

More than anything else, a clear focus on core mission is vital for successful, faith-based social innovation and redemptive entrepreneurship. As a redemptive entrepreneur, you cannot expect funders, either in the form of donors or investors, to give you money if you are not clear about your mission; and if they do, that money will have less impact as it gets diluted by nonessential activity. This may seem obvious, but it is not always easy to keep focus on the road ahead. It is all too common for organizations to head off course chasing funding or because something "seems like a good idea." In the realm of social innovation and ministry, there are always more needs and good ideas than there are time and resources for a single organization to address.

When Erica and I moved to Madison to begin our work rebuilding Pres House, a lot was missing. There were zero students, the building was run-down, and there was not enough funding to pay for our salaries and other expenses. But among the "somethings" that we did have was clarity in direction. The board of directors knew where they wanted to go. They wanted to relaunch and grow an active, thriving campus ministry to undergraduate and graduate students, build an apartment community on the parking lot, renovate the seventy-five-year-old chapel building, and develop a funding plan to cover the expenses of a comprehensive campus ministry center on an ongoing basis. They wanted to completely rebuild and reshape Pres House for decades to come. The vision was bold. It was challenging.

In all honesty, when Erica and I were interviewing for the position at Pres House, we had very little idea what we were getting ourselves into or how we were going to carry out the vision of the board. But we knew one thing for sure—it was going to take some time to realize the vision. We asked the board to commit to us and the effort for at least seven years, and we agreed to do the same. We knew that the destination we had in mind was many miles away and that it would take years of pedaling for us to reach it. We took a long view with our eyes fixed on where we were going.

What did that look like practically? It meant that we thought about and described Pres House, not as it was, but as it would be. We talked about Pres House as a full-fledged, thriving campus ministry—even before it actually was. We spoke its future into existence. We put aside the cheap newsletters and brochures made in-house on a small printer and started producing professional-quality publications. Why? Because that is where we were going. That is the level of organization we were becoming. We redesigned the website, cleaned up the building, created a new logo, made new signs—all to signal to ourselves and others that Pres House was going somewhere and was going to be something. And we stayed laser-focused on the vision for the future by saying no to more things than we said yes to.

We have had to say no to a great idea at least once a week for the roughly eight hundred weeks we've been at Pres House. For the first year of our ministry, we said no to all programming. Instead of organizing activities or hosting events, we made a commitment to spend an entire year learning about what was happening on campus, getting connected with our board and other leaders in the area, and listening to students and their needs. We said no to partnerships that were no longer moving Pres House in the right direction. We even said no to ideas that board members thought we should try right away.

This didn't make everyone happy, but it is a big part of how we got to where we are today. We kept our eyes on the road ahead.

In any organization there is always another good and important thing to be done. There are countless good ideas out there, infinite causes worth supporting, endless options for how to spend energy, time, and money. But many of these ideas are side streets, detours from the real direction you are headed. You will go where you are looking. Don't look down at where you are now. That will leave you wobbling along and not getting very far. Instead, look up and ahead to where you want to be. Don't take side streets that pull you off course. Say no to the things that are not moving you in the right direction. Don't focus on the obstacles in the way. Obstacles will come up, and you'll have to ride around them or maybe through them. But if you focus on those potholes, you'll get stuck in them. Look ahead to where you want to be.

Staying true to core mission is especially vital when dealing with the finances of redemptive entrepreneurship and social enterprise. Funding social innovation is a constant and serious challenge. It takes much hard work, creativity, and resilience to seek funding, to get back up after being told no, and to put all the pieces together to make the finances work. But beware of the danger of devoting too much energy toward financial increase without clear regard for mission. It is easy to chase funding where it is available or to make decisions based on money first and mission second. The drive for money, especially more money, is a powerful force. Just because we engage in mission-focused work doesn't mean we will be immune to the siren call of making money for the sake of making money. If a social enterprise becomes driven first by money, over and above fulfilling mission, the tail has begun wagging the dog.

Mark Sampson warns that social enterprise can be so fully co-opted by mainstream economic language and thinking that it doesn't offer anything new or life giving to the world. Sampson suggests that if social enterprise doesn't offer something different from traditional business, a more faithful economic practice, and a more humanizing approach to market forces, then it is missing its true promise.[2] This may happen even if we don't intend it to. Thus are the power and peril of our traditional economic framework.

I am encouraged that, in recent research about congregational-based social enterprise, "congregational leaders indicate that their primary motivation is to advance what they see as their congregation's underlying mission," and not to generate revenue (although that is also part of the motivation in many cases).[3] This is how it should be.

At Pres House, we have had to make some hard decisions about funding in order to keep our eyes on the road ahead. Many of those decisions came during construction of Pres House Apartments. It is often stated that when building a large facility like a seven-story apartment building, the owner makes about one million decisions. From room layout, to paint colors, to construction materials, there were so many decisions. And some decisions had important mission implications for us. One such decision was about the design and use of common space in the building.

It was vital that the project, once open, work financially (more detail on this later). We had only one shot at constructing this building, and we had only one piece of property to build on. We had to be as sure as we could that once the building was operational, the finances would work and the weight of construction costs and debt would not pull the organization under. And so we needed to maximize the amount of revenue that could be produced by the space we were designing and building.

But at the same time, we were not building apartments primarily to make money. We were building them to provide a unique and

2. Mark Sampson, "The Promise of Social Enterprise: A Theological Exploration of Faithful Economic Practice" (PhD diss., King's College London, 2019), 13–14.

3. Thad Austin, "Social Entrepreneurship among Protestant American Congregations: The Role, Theology, Motivations, and Experiences of Lay and Clergy Leadership" (PhD diss., Indiana University, 2019), 173.

transformative living community in which students could thrive and be supported. At a certain point in our design conversations, the need for financial performance conflicted with the core mission. We really wanted a lot of community lounge and recreation room space in the apartment building for students to interact with each other and access programs. Even though each apartment had a full kitchen and living room, it was vital for our mission that there be common spaces throughout the building as well.

Most apartment buildings designed for maximum revenue generation do not have much common space. In a typical student housing facility, you enter a small lobby where there may be mailboxes and perhaps a leasing office, while the rest of the building is income-producing space. But we decided to put common lounges on each floor and a large multipurpose room on the main level. We could easily have fit many more income-producing rooms in the spaces that we set aside as common space. This mission-focused decision cost us significant financial performance. It was not an easy decision. It led to serious arguments among our internal team of staff, volunteers, and consultants. But it was the right decision. Our common space is used all the time for programs that we run and that students host for each other. It also sets us apart from traditional student housing.

We faced another difficult mission and money decision just a few years ago. We were extremely honored to be invited to apply for a major, invitation-only grant from a prominent foundation. The grant would have likely been for almost $1 million. But we turned down the offer. We felt the grant program, while valuable, exciting, and needed in the larger ecosystem, was not the right fit for Pres House at the time. We felt it would pull us too far off course from who we are and what we are called to do and be. While good work, it would have redirected major energy and time away from our core mission. You can imagine the interesting conversation generated at our board meeting when I said, "We have been invited to apply for a major grant, but I recommend we should say no." After extensive prayer and discussion, our board of directors agreed. We turned down the opportunity.

That difficult decision turned out to be the right one. By staying focused, we were able to continue to grow the reach and impact of our core mission during the years we would have been working on the grant project. And the decision ultimately increased our credibility in the eyes of the foundation. They eventually funded a new program that was much more in line with our mission with a different grant. By keeping our eyes on the road ahead, we did not deviate from our course by taking even that worthy and meaningful side street.

## Measure and Manage Impact Outcomes

One of the ways that redemptive entrepreneurs can be sure they are staying focused on their core mission is by measuring and managing desired impact outcomes. Impact measurement gets a lot of discussion in the social business and nonprofit sectors. Seventy-five percent of charities measure some or all of their work, and nearly three-quarters have invested more in measuring results over the last five years.[4] There is less emphasis on this in the church environment, partly because it is exceedingly hard to measure outcomes in many of the areas that church institutions work. How, for example, does one measure spiritual growth? The church, if it measures anything at all, has resorted to counting bodies and bucks—the number of people showing up in the pews and dollars given to the church. But these are output measurements, not outcome measurements. Although counting the number of people who show up to a service or program, or counting the number of programs offered, may serve a useful purpose, most of the time it simply measures the amount of activity taking place and not the change that occurs in people's lives. More people attending does not necessarily mean more people influenced.

4. Tris Lumley, "Raising the Bar on Nonprofit Impact Measurement," *Stanford Social Innovation Review*, July 10, 2013, https://ssir.org/articles/entry/raising_the _bar_on_nonprofits_impact_measurement.

I often joke that if we wanted to increase attendance at Pres House, we would only need to roll out a couple of kegs of beer onto our patio on a Friday night and we would "succeed" in getting a huge crowd. But getting lots of people to show up doesn't mean that we are serving our core mission of promoting the spiritual, emotional, and intellectual growth of students. So, rather than roll out beer to increase our *output*, we have actually begun cosponsoring a Sober Tailgate party on football weekends to support students in addiction recovery—a truly *outcome*-focused program.

In fact, we have done a lot of work at Pres House in recent years trying to clarify the outcomes we are measuring in order to keep to our core mission. For, as the saying goes, "what gets measured, gets done." At Pres House, we have identified five outcomes that more fully describe what "spiritual, emotional, and intellectual growth" looks like in the lives of students and young adults. Our five objectives are:

1. Help students develop a deeper and more mature faith.
2. Offer students an experience of gracious welcome and connection.
3. Invite, identify, and share student gifts in, and outside, of Pres House.
4. Improve the capacity for students to interact with people different from themselves.
5. Help students cultivate wellness in community.

We have then set about establishing specific, measurable outcomes in each of these areas. For example, we try to track the number of other Pres House residents each resident gets to know from when they move into the building in the fall to when they leave in the spring. Our goal is for 85 percent of residents to at least double the number of other residents they know by the end of the school year. This measurement helps us pinpoint the outcome we are looking for—that we are offering students an experience of connection.

Another goal is that 90 percent of those who participate in the student church at Pres House have opportunities through Pres House to interact with people different from themselves. We believe connecting across racial/ethnic, gender identification, sexual orientation, and other lines is vital to what it means to grow spiritually.

Measurement of impact outcomes is vital for staying focused on core mission. It helps employees and volunteers all row in the same direction and ensures that money and energy are spent on the things that matter and not on the things that don't. And if done right, measurement turns into management. Sometimes organizations do measure and count but then don't use the acquired information to change or manage differently for better outcomes. If measurement is done only to keep track of what is happening, and not to change anything about activities, process, or programs, then we have missed a great deal of the value of measurement. As Morgan Simon notes, "achieving the ultimate goal, of course, requires knowing how to manage, not just measure."[5]

Impact measurement is particularly important when impact investment is part of the funding of social enterprise. Blended value says that the return on an impact investment is a blend of the financial return and the social return. The financial return is relatively easy to measure by counting dollars and cents. The social return is much harder to quantify. But we must try to at least describe, if not ideally quantify in some way, the social impact such investments are making in the world.

At Pres House, we pay the Synod of Lakes and Prairies a fixed 4.6 percent financial return on their impact investment. But we also provide a social return in the lives of thousands of students. Our outcome measurement, while not converted into dollars and cents in most cases, is a critical part of the blended value we provide our investors and donors. And in some cases, we are able to translate our impact into financial terms. For example, our Next Step Sober

---

5. Morgan Simon, *Real Impact: The New Economics of Social Change* (New York: Nation Books, 2017), 142.

housing program has saved Wisconsin about half a million dollars in relapse-related costs in the past few years.

This sort of measurement is not easy to do in social services and particularly in the church. And it should not be sought after obsessively. We always try to keep our data tracking and measurement in service of the larger mission and not let them become, or distract from, the purpose. We are in the business of transformation, not measuring things. Measurement must serve ministry, not the other way around.

One of the most effective ways we've found to broaden our understanding of the outcomes our programs have in people's lives is through storytelling. While storytelling may not produce graphs and traditional data-driven measurement, it is a powerful way to describe what is happening through redemptive entrepreneurship. At Pres House, we intentionally collect and share stories of transformation from participants in our programs to ensure that people are not just showing up but are being changed for the better by their experiences at Pres House. Collecting stories with no "hard data" isn't enough, but at the same time, collecting "data without stories is soulless."[6]

## Make It Work—Attend to the Business Model

It is vital for successful faith-based social innovation in which impact investing can play a role to stay focused on the core mission. One of the best tools for doing that is clearly identifying impact outcomes, measuring them, and managing to reach them. That is what this work is all about, after all—transformation in lives.

But if mission is one side of the coin, then the *business of mission* is the other side. As mentioned above, when we designed the physical layout of the Pres House Apartments building, we had to make the finances of the

6. Todd Johnson, "Welcome to iPAR," *Medium*, March 22, 2019, https://medium .com/@todd_94277/welcome-to-ipar-b84227525f9d.

project work. It would not have served our mission at all to build a facility with a business model that would have resulted in financial ruin.

I often encounter leaders in the church who resist conversations about business. "Isn't ministry all about relationships with God and people?" "The church isn't a business, so why should we spend energy on budgets, facilities, and operations?" "Can't we just 'love on people'?"

I understand those questions. And I resonate with the sense of unease that many in the church and nonprofit world experience when talking about revenue, marketing, investments, and so on. The church is not a business. Ministry is all about relationships and serving people and neighborhoods. "Business is not ministry when the business interferes with sacred acts or creates a barrier for others to encounter God."[7] The treasures in heaven that we care about are people—not money or buildings or websites. We care about people.

But if we don't attend to the "business" of mission, our mission will not be effective. Put another way, if the business is managed and run well, then the real work of mission is much more fruitful. The business operation of a nonprofit or ministry is its skeleton. If the skeleton is strong, then the flesh that is laid on top of it—the programs, the people, the relationships—flourishes, and the organization succeeds. So, yes, we do this work in order to love and serve people. But we have to tend to the business in order for our work with people to, well, work!

The Home Community Cafe is a social enterprise started by a community of people living in Earlsfield, a neighborhood in London, England. The café is run out of St. Andrew's Church in the center of Earlsfield. The café space is in the back half of the church sanctuary—a unique way of approaching this sort of venture. It is open Monday to Friday and closed on the weekend so that traditional activities and services can take place in the church. But during the weekday hours during which a church is often empty,

7. Austin, "Social Entrepreneurship," 120.

this space is full of people eating, connecting, and engaging in events that promote creative arts, life skills, health and well-being, and friendship. Organized as a Community Interest Company, a designation available in the United Kingdom, Home Cafe benefits the community, the local residents of Earlsfield. As described on their website, "The coffee shop and multi-use community space is a place that is open to all, equipping, empowering and encouraging our local community to explore and develop its potential."

I had a chance to visit Home Cafe in the summer of 2018 and meet the folks who started it. They felt it was important to engage with food in community because they view the New Testament as fundamentally about the core question: "Who do I eat with?" Food is economic, political, and social. It touches all aspects of life. One of the founders commented, "If you get food right, you may start to get other things right." They are intentional about not approaching the venture as if they have answers or gifts to give, but as people who are part of the community and are invested in its well-being.

The owner of the business, Meg, talked about the constant balance between keeping focus on core mission and ensuring financial viability, between being profitable and helping people. One of the specific ways they have addressed this balance is by using the tips given by customers to subsidize food that they give away. That way they can sell their food at close to market-rate prices, make the business model work, and still provide free food to those that need it by repurposing the tips from customers for mission. It was clear in talking with those who founded and run Home Cafe that they are practicing a constant balancing act.

Here's another bike analogy. I hang out with college students at the University of Wisconsin–Madison. They often use bikes to get around our large campus. Even in the sub-zero temperatures and snow-covered roads of winter! I am often dismayed by how poorly many students take care of their bikes. They leave them outside, uncovered in the snow, for months at a time. They ride to class with totally flat tires. And they almost never, ever oil their chain. You can always tell when a bike needs some oil on its chain by the horrible creaking and grinding sound it makes as it goes by. These same students often wonder why it is so hard to ride to class and are shocked that I ride sixty miles before 9 a.m. each Wednesday.

But I treat my chain and bike very differently than they treat theirs. I clean and lube my chain almost every day. I pump up my tires every time I take my bike outside. I change my cables, bar tape, brake pads, and tires multiple times per season. If I had an orange rusty chain on my bike, I'd find it hard to ride a mile to class, too. One must take care of a bike for it to work well. If the chain is rusty or your tires are full of holes, you won't make it very far, and you'll end up spending all your time dealing with the problems with the bike rather than riding anywhere. In addition to offering the gracious welcome of God to students, I often feel like an evangelist for bike maintenance!

The big picture is important, but it is also essential to attend to the little details that make a huge difference. Loving people is the purpose of ministry. But we must also put oil on the chain and pump up the tires. We must take care of the "business" of ministry. If the operation is rusty and the business has holes in it, then the mission will not go anywhere, or we will end up stopped on the side of the road, changing a flat tire instead of getting on with loving people. I don't oil the chain on my bike so that I have a shiny chain; I oil the chain so that my bike works well and I can get to where I am going. In the same way, I don't attend to the business of Pres House just so we run a "well-oiled machine"; I attend to the business so that our mission of transforming the lives of students is successful and we get to where we are going.

Let me share a few examples:

- We try to run the best student-housing community on campus with excellent customer service, cleanliness, and amenities so that students want to live with us and will have the opportunity to experience the grace of Jesus Christ as members of our residential community.

- We send handwritten thank-you notes to every donor, after every donation, because we want our relationship with our donors to extend beyond the online transaction or check they write.
- We produce high-quality newsletters, annual reports, and other publications so that people can clearly see what we are about and be inspired to participate in and support our work.
- We are always looking for ways to improve our computer systems, databases, phone systems, sound systems, and facilities so that our people and programs can flourish and do their best work.
- We engage in rigorous financial modeling and budgeting in order to best leverage the gifts that God has given us for our mission today and into the future.
- We take surveys throughout the year and collect data on all our programming to evaluate what we are doing and to make changes to be more effective.

Most of all, the business model has to work. In addition, to do the work of our social mission, the finances have to work. Like the other ingredients that apply to all faith-based social innovation projects, this is particularly important for those social enterprises that are looking to use impact investment to finance growth or operations. For an organization to provide a financial return to an investor, that organization needs a successful enough business model to cover all costs, have funds for growth, and have enough left over to pay out that financial return. This is true if the organization is structured as a for-profit social enterprise or a nonprofit.

A faith-based social enterprise can generate funds in a number of ways. I'll summarize them in three large buckets:

1. *Contributed income* provides the majority of funding for many nonprofit organizations. This is money given to an organization

with no expectation that anything will be paid back. This takes the form of individual donations, grants, bequests, and other gifts. At Pres House, we receive contributed income from alumni donors, foundations, parents, student members, and other committed donors who support the services we provide. Because of our business model, 100 percent of money donated to Pres House goes directly to student programming and services.

2.   *Earned income* can apply to nonprofit and for-profit social enterprises alike. It is derived from selling products or services. A well-known example is the YMCA, which sells gym memberships to the public as a major source of funding and then uses that income, along with contributed income, to provide other services for the community, much of it for free or at below market-rate cost. At Pres House, our residents pay to live in the Pres House Apartments, and all of that earned income funds our operation and the services we provide to residents. Churches have begun joining other nonprofit organizations in experimenting with earned income through social enterprise. As traditional giving from the collection plate declines, it makes sense to explore ministry activities that also generate revenue through a sale of goods or services.

3.   *Investments* are the third source of funds. If a social enterprise can demonstrate a strong business model in generating contributed and earned income, then investors may be willing to make debt or equity investments in the organization. Equity investments take a partial ownership stake in the organization, while debt investments lend money to an organization expecting the principal to be paid back with interest. There are many ways the specifics of these investments can be designed.

Kathleen Kelly Janus offers very helpful observations about the financial operation of nonprofit organizations in her book *Social Startup Success*. Her research indicates that "successfully developing an earned-income strategy was one of the ways organizations broke through the $2 million annual revenue barrier."[8] While some needs cannot be met by selling something, and some services must be given away for free, long-term financial sustainability often comes to organizations that are able to develop some kind of earned-income strategy. Those looking to engage impact investors will almost certainly have to design a "profitable" earned-income strategy.[9]

Janus also found that most of the long-term sustainable nonprofits whose budgets grew past $3 million eventually pursued one primary source of funding.[10] It is common practice in nonprofit fund-raising to diversify funding sources and not rely on one source for too much of the overall budget. This is prudent; if a major grant is lost, and that is the majority funding source, then an organization is much more likely to fail. And it is true that the majority of organizations under the $3 million size will rely on a variety of funding sources. But those that grow larger and stick around for a long time tend to settle into a model that preferences one kind of funding over the others. They develop core competency in generating that specific kind of money.

This has been true for us at Pres House. We generate most of our revenue from earned income associated with our program services, namely, students renting in the Pres House Apartments. We have focused our energy and developed skills in doing this successfully. It is still essential, however, that we also raise contributed income from donors and foundations to provide vital revenue for programming. Rather than a funding pie cut into five or six equal slices of income, our pie has one very large slice and a few smaller slices making up an effective whole that works very well. Regardless of the number of pieces of your pie and how the funding is derived, you need to attend to the business of your mission and make sure that the financial model works.

<hr />

8. Kathleen Kelly Janus, *Social Startup Success: How the Best Nonprofits Launch, Scale Up, and Make a Difference* (New York: De Capo Lifelong Books, 2017), 93.

9. There is nothing preventing a nonprofit from generating revenue or "profit." What nonprofits cannot do is pass along that profit to an individual or set of individuals such as owners or shareholders. All "profit" must be used for operation and mission purposes.

10. Janus, *Social Startup Success*, 96.

## Align Money and Mission

Mission is primary. Money is also important. Both need to be attended to for successful social enterprise or redemptive entrepreneurship to happen. The most fruitful scenario is when the two come together as one integrated whole. Money and mission. Mission and money. This is where impact investing in the church has the most potential to work beautifully. At Pres House we were fortunate to find a way to bring these two together for powerful outcomes.

I use a version of this map with my board and staff to help us think about how we align money and mission in our organization. We evaluate our activities and programs based on where they fall on this map.

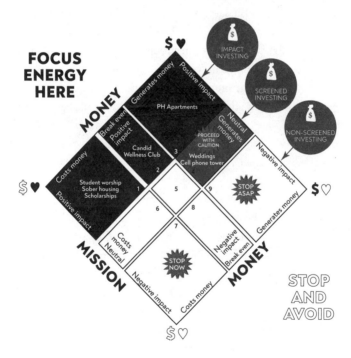

Activities that fall in along the upper left on this diamond (the black boxes) have positive mission impact. Those in the middle are neutral—they neither contribute to nor detract from our mission impact. Those in the bottom third have a negative mission impact—they are harmful to the mission of the organization or to what we want to see happen in the world.

In a similar way we can map the financial impact as we move along on the map. Activities and programs that fall along the upper right side generate money. They have a net positive financial impact on the organization. Those in the middle third basically break even. And those in the lower left have a net negative financial impact. They cost us more money than they bring in. By mapping what we do into one of these nine boxes we can evaluate the overall impact of our activity on the mission and financial resiliency of our organization. We can see where money and mission align and where they do not.

The activities on the far left, box 1, have a high, positive mission impact and are central to our mission. We do these things because they are core to our mission even though they cost us more money than they bring in. Holding worship experiences for students and giving away scholarships for residents in sober housing fall into this category. While many students are generous, they do not give enough in the offering plate to fund our Sunday worship gatherings. We conduct them anyway, however, because they are core to our mission. We must engage in activities in another area of the map to generate revenue and fund these programs.

The activities in the gray box 4 generate revenue to support those that lose money in box 1. They have no real positive or negative mission impact, but they bring in money to fund other activities. In our case at Pres House we lease some space on our roof to a cell phone provider. There is nothing negative about that activity, but neither does it contribute to our mission. We aren't in the business of providing four bars of cell service to people walking past our building. It is mission neutral. But the positive income stream covers scholarships for students to take service-learning trips over winter break and attend retreats for wellness and spiritual growth.

Notice that five of the nine boxes are white. These are activities that have neutral or negative mission impact. Why are we doing them if they don't have positive mission impact? Especially if they also don't generate any revenue? It is clear that if something we are doing has a negative impact and doesn't generate any money, we should stop doing that. But what about activities that have no real positive or negative mission impact and cost money or just break even? A surprising number of activities fall into these boxes in many congregations and nonprofits. We've had to change or eliminate a number of activities at Pres House to get out of these boxes.

And what about activities that make us money but have a negative impact? As noted earlier in this book, certain investments fall into this category. If we are making money from investments in weapons manufacturers Monday through Friday while preaching about peace and the value of human life on Sunday, then our investment strategy falls into box 9. This can be a particularly tricky space to be in for mission-focused organizations, especially if the financial returns are high. We have to be really honest about where revenue is coming from in case it falls in this space. The goal is to move completely out of box 9 over time.

This tool has generated very interesting conversations over the years. For example, we place the use of our chapel for weddings in box 4. Weddings provide some financial benefit from renting the space, but most of them are low in mission impact for us. This might seem counterintuitive at first. Isn't using a chapel space for a wedding service a core mission of a faith-based organization like Pres House? In our case it is not. We exist to serve students at the University of Wisconsin–Madison. When students from our community want to get married at Pres House, their wedding is core to our mission. But it is not a part of our core mission to rent the chapel to members of the general public who want to get married in a pretty church space. It is a nice use of the space. There is nothing wrong with it. But it isn't core to who we are. Even though we are a faith-based organization with a physical chapel, hosting a Sober Tailgate party outside or wellness cooking classes in our kitchen is often more aligned with our mission than a wedding held in the chapel. We want to keep our eyes on the road ahead and not get distracted by something that seems like what churches are supposed to do but is actually a side street.

This raises fascinating questions about the core purpose of faith-based organizations, even of congregations. How do we best serve the needs of our communities? Is it always through church services that happen in a sanctuary? Or could there be more vital and aligned ways for us to connect the good news of the gospel with people's everyday lives? Could it be that some different expressions of "church" are actually more closely associated with the core mission of our organizations than the programs and activities we have offered in past decades? Perhaps a social enterprise is a better use of time, money, and space than a traditional Bible study. Clarity around core mission is the first essential step to aligning money and mission effectively.

Sacred Space is a coworking and event space housed in a Nazarene church in Palo Alto, California. A creative, missional-minded entrepreneur, Brandon Napoli, renovated the fellowship hall and classrooms in the church to create a welcoming space for other Silicon Valley entrepreneurs. They describe their mission as follows: "Creating time, relationships, and purpose to flourish, Sacred Space is a drop-in work space for our neighbors to focus on their passions, while feeling grounded and connecting with a community of like-minded individuals. We focus on women, impact entrepreneurs, artists, and transitional workers. Our space provides business and educational services, day care, and spiritual formation for productivity, hospitality, and creativity."[11] Payment is made on a donation basis. Coworking is available Monday to

11. https://sacredspace.io/.

Friday so that the space is available to the church for weekend services and activities.

Sacred Space has found a niche serving women who are able to use the day-care center that is also run out of the church. By opening up their space for a very different purpose than what churches usually use their fellowship hall for, Sacred Space is able to engage people who have rarely, if ever, set foot in church. They are able to break down barriers of distrust and open up conversations with a much wider network of people than traditional church services were doing. Income from the coworking rental helps fund their activities.

It is the activities in boxes 2 and 3 of the mission/money chart that are most important for those considering impact investment and sustainable social innovation. These activities serve the core mission *and* generate revenue either by paying for themselves as in box 2 or generating surplus revenue as in box 3. At Pres House, the Pres House Apartments sit right at the tip of the diamond in box 3. Providing a unique housing option for students at the University of Wisconsin–Madison is central to our mission and has been a dream since the founding of the organization. We serve more students, more deeply, through the Pres House Apartments than in almost anything else we do as an organization. At the same time the Pres House Apartments provide the most robust and sustainable revenue source that we have as an organization. The better we run our apartment community, the better outcomes we have in the lives of students and the better outcomes we have financially. Mission and financial impact rise in sync in the Pres House Apartments.

Ted Levinson, the founder of Beneficial Returns, an impact-investing fund that leverages donor-advised fund money for social impact in developing countries, describes this as the defining feature of social enterprise. "The more revenue they generate the more good they do. It's not ancillary to their work—it *is* their work."[12] He gives the example of Guayakí, a social business that Beneficial Returns invests in. Guayakí started in 1996 with a goal of protecting 200,000 acres of South American rainforest while also creating over one thousand living-wage jobs—all before the year 2020. Guayakí achieves this goal through the sale of yerba mate beverages that are distributed widely throughout the United States. They work with indigenous cooperatives that supply them with yerba mate. The farmers have an incentive to preserve, and even restore, the rainforest, for yerba mate naturally grows under tree cover in Brazil, Argentina, and Paraguay. Ultimately, the more drinks Guayakí sells at 7-Eleven convenience stores, Safeway, and other outlets, the more acreage of the rainforest is protected. The more successful they are with production and sales, the more money they make and the more impact they generate.[13]

Finding this sweet spot is not always easy or even possible in redemptive entrepreneurship. But where it can be designed, there is potential for enormous impact. This is a powerful way to merge the two pockets and integrate money and mission. Impact investment works best where high mission outcomes are matched with high financial outcomes. And this alignment can help with the other ingredients. As authors from the Harvard Business School and Echoing Green point out, "the best way to limit the tug of mission drift is to run a business venture directly related to your social mission and integral to furthering it."[14] They call this the "hybrid ideal."

So, how can we do more as a church to shift our activities on the mission/money map? What hybrid ideals can we envision? Even small steps will pay major financial and mission dividends.

12. From email exchange with Ted Levinson on July 11, 2019.

13. From 2018 Beneficial Returns Annual Report and email exchange with Ted Levinson, July 2019.

14. Julie Battilana et al., "In Search of the Hybrid Ideal," *Stanford Social Innovation Review*, Summer 2012, https://ssir.org/articles/entry/in_search_of_the_hybrid _ideal#.

## Embrace Risk and Failure

When I talk to people and groups about the story of Pres House, there are often gasps of surprise when I get to the part of the story where we borrowed $17 million to build the Pres House Apartments. This number is tiny for some organizations and in some sectors. But for a Presbyterian campus ministry with an annual budget of $150,000, that was a huge sum of money. And it remains a large amount for many nonprofit social enterprises, especially those in the church. While nonprofit organizations are often willing to take risks in providing program services, they are much more risk-averse when it comes to financial matters.[15]

Borrowing $17 million was a huge risk. In many ways it still is. Although we have paid down some of the principal, we still owe more millions than I want to think about. If we aren't vigilant with marketing, upkeep, managing costs, tracking interest rates, and many other factors, the finances of our operation could easily unravel. And many of the risks are out of our control. During the financial crisis of fall 2008 and the beginning of the COVID-19 pandemic in spring 2020, our interest rates went through the roof, and there was nothing we could do about it.

But despite the fear and uncertainty, our board of directors was willing to embrace risk when we set out to transform the organization. It even pushed us to articulate risk taking as a primary operating principle of the organization.

During our first year on the job when we were especially green and naive, Erica and I brought a set of primary operating principles to our board of directors to guide us in the how we went about building a renewed organization. We felt it would help guide our work to name and describe the way we were going to go about our ministry. The three principles we first articulated were as follows:

*We embrace change.* What we do this year may not work next year, probably won't work in five years, and almost certainly won't work

---

15. Austin, "Social Entrepreneurship," 79.

in ten years. Rather than commit ourselves to programs and systems that work for now and then struggle to try to change them in the future, we build change into everything we do. As a Presbyterian-based organization, we say that we are reformed and always being reformed (while being firmly committed to our mission!).

*We welcome those skeptical or otherwise "outside" the church.* We welcome all students, including committed Christians, but we are not interested in just attracting the same small group of already devoted students who move from ministry to ministry. We are home for Presbyterian students, but we desire to reach students of any and all backgrounds. There are almost forty thousand students at the University of Wisconsin–Madison, and only a small fraction are involved in a church or campus ministry. Reaching the "nones and dones" requires us to think creatively, act proactively, and minimize barriers to entry.

*We understand and embrace where God is at work in the university.* The current student culture is very different from that of generations past. The gospel has not changed, but the people to whom we are taking it have. Rather than try to change students to be like us, we seek to translate the gospel in a way that is relevant to them. We strive to use programs, activities, sermon examples, and structures that are indigenous to students at UW–Madison. Rather than approaching the university as a dark, scary, godless place, we seek to identify and lift up the many incredible ways in which God is already at work in and through the university. Rather than taking an antagonistic approach to what is taught in the classroom, we seek to help students integrate their faith with their studies.

In the midst of all the things we got totally wrong in the early years, and all the many places we had no idea what we were doing, this one we got right. These principles have turned out to be a vital and abiding guide for us all at Pres House. We still use them today, and students tell us that they reflect accurately who we are as an organization.

But there was one key principle missing that our board of directors pointed out right away. So we added it:

*We embrace risk.* Everything we do at Pres House is risky. Borrowing $17 million was risky. Building a major student-housing project was risky. Starting a new worship service from scratch was risky. But the risks we take are necessary, considered, and reasonable. We need to take risks because the alternative is certain, slow death. We risk in faith, believing that we are participating in God's work on campus and at Pres House. And we do it all thoughtfully and prayerfully with eyes wide open, striving to be good stewards of our resources and making decisions with as much good information as possible.

This final principle has been perhaps the most important over the last fifteen years and plays a role in all our decisions. Embrace risk, said the board, because we cannot do this innovative work without taking risks to do things differently.

One more cycling analogy: One of the most counterintuitive aspects of balancing on a bike is that the faster you go, the easier it is to balance. The temptation when starting out riding is to be cautious, to go slow, to keep one hand on the brake. But doing this makes the likelihood of falling much greater than if you simply let go of the brake and go. As the bike speeds up, it becomes easier to balance. To ride successfully, you must take the risk, trust the physics of the bike, release the brake, fully commit, and pedal forward. For most children who have initially mastered two wheels, the hardest part of riding becomes the start and the stop—when the bike is moving slowly. This is also why you see bike commuters slow down at stop signs but not always completely stop. It is hard to get going again, and the chance of falling down is highest when riding slowly.

The same is true in social innovation and redemptive entrepreneurship—especially when leading birth, growth, or change. As Albert Einstein quipped, "Life is like riding a bicycle. To keep your balance you must keep moving."[16] We cannot expect to launch successful social enterprises if we have one hand on the brake the whole time.

16. Albert Einstein, letter to his son Edward, February 5, 1930, in *Words to Ride By:*

I have seen too many churches try to start a new ministry project with a $5,000 grant, insist that the youth program budget be limited to the funds raised at an annual pancake breakfast, or avoid trying a new program because something similar failed ten years earlier. Yes, careful, prudent planning is vital, but trying to get riding while being so overly cautious dooms the project to crash and fail before it even has a chance to get started.

I have a good friend who recently launched a new company in Silicon Valley that develops digital tools to help people pray. His business spent more than $400,000 in its first year of operation. And that was well below the average cost of launching a tech start-up. It takes major investment and a willingness to take risks to start something new.

At Pres House, we embrace risk. We are thoughtful about our risk taking. We run seven-year financial projections to try to anticipate the future. We engage in rigorous program evaluation, fund development, and strategic planning. We recognize that everything we try may not work and some things will fail. But we are committed to letting go of the brake and making a real go of it.

What does this look like in practice? At Pres House, we spent over half a million dollars more than we brought in during the first five years of our rebirth. We hired the staff we needed to launch a new worshiping community, quadruple our database of donors, and manage a rapidly growing organization. And we paid them competitive wages. We invested in good, quality computers, website development, and database software.

Letting go of the brakes isn't only about taking financial risks. We took a risk to engage members more actively in worship by changing our seating from rows of pews to small clusters of chairs. We tried programs that we thought people would love but nobody showed up to. And we tried programs that we thought nobody would show

---

*Thoughts on Bicycling,* by Michael Carabetta (San Francisco: Chronicle Books 2017), 67.

up to but people loved. The truth is that every one of these decisions could have led to failure (and still could today, or in the future). Some of them did. We could have crashed and burned, and we came close many times in the past decade. We did fall down at times, and it was (and is) terrifying.

But we have tried to reframe failure as learning. And learning is essential for social innovation. If we hadn't taken these risks, if we had kept one hand on the brake, we would have certainly failed. A halfhearted effort would have sputtered and died before it had a chance to really thrive. The greatest gift the board of directors gave Pres House was a willingness to invest fully in the effort, to take risks, and to really go for it.

Perhaps most importantly, we gained momentum. When we let go of the brakes and start to roll faster, we pick up speed and momentum. Participants and outside observers see what is happening and want to be a part of it. Student leaders catch on that they can try new things, and that energizes them. Donors get excited and want to give to successful programs. In 2004, donors were giving $10,000 per year to Pres House. After letting go of the brakes, we have raised more than $5 million in the years since. The bike is really moving now.

Let go of the brakes. Don't hold back for fear of failure. Doing so will be a self-fulfilling prophecy, and your wobbly bike will fall. Go for it! Commit fully. Trust that God will do great things. And if what you try doesn't work, if your bike gets out of control and you crash—trust that God remains bigger than that, too. We don't serve a God who wants us to bury our talent in the ground and play it safe. We don't serve a God who punishes risk taking or failure. We serve a God who is so much bigger than even our grandest ideas or dreams. So let go of the brakes and ride!

# 11

## *Ingredients to Make It Work for Investors*

In the previous chapter I explored key ingredients for redemptive entrepreneurs and program leaders to consider when engaging in social enterprise, especially social enterprise funded by impact investment. I will now turn to the other side of the coin—investors. What ingredients do investors need to keep in mind in order to encourage social impact, effectively fund redemptive entrepreneurship, and earn a fair and reasonable return on their assets?

When I speak of investors here, I am first thinking of church-related institutions, foundations, and endowments that have investment or property capital to redeploy into redemptive entrepreneurship as investors. This could be denominational foundations, denominational judicatories, pension funds, seminaries, church-related colleges, churches, or other institutions with investable assets or property. These ingredients would equally apply to individual church members interested in using personal capital to make a difference through impact investing.

Even those of us with few to no investment assets of our own are connected to institutions that do have resources. Churches we worship at, colleges we attended, businesses we work for, banks we use—all these institutions have some connection to resources. As Morgan Simon points out, "just about everyone in the United States has some connection to an institution investing at least $1 billion." Which means, "at a certain level we are all billionaires when it comes to influencing where money goes in the economy."[1]

---

1. Morgan Simon, *Real Impact: The New Economics of Social Change* (New York: Nation Books, 2017), 24.

## Look for People and Organizations on the Margins
## That Are Making a Difference

Redemptive entrepreneurship has a long tradition in the church. Monks have grown food and brewed beer to sustain their communities for centuries. Churches started schools and hospitals to provide vital needs in communities. Church-related colleges, camps, senior housing, and now student housing are all ways of serving communities while generating revenue. African American church communities have run credit unions for members for decades. There are 133 active credit unions with a faith-based charter in the United States currently.

In 1965 the Greater Galilee Missionary Baptist Church in Milwaukee started a credit union for its predominantly African American membership. Milwaukee is one of the most racially segregated cities in the nation. African American residents were, and still are, regularly denied loans, lines of credit, and other financial services. The church-founded credit union serves two hundred members and others associated with them. The credit union is run separately from the church, but it is housed in the basement of the congregation's building. Unlike a bank that exists to generate returns for investors and owners, a credit union is a not-for-profit financial entity that exists to provide financial services to its members. Many of the members of Greater Galilee Credit Union do not have ready access to financial services from other institutions. Without their credit union, they would have to turn to predatory payday lenders for access to loans. While serving members with their services, Greater Galilee Credit Union must also negotiate the complex regulatory environment of the banking business and generate enough revenue to stay in business.[2]

2. Katelyn Ferral, "Church-Run Credit Unions Keep the Faith Despite Chal-

But much of the work of redemptive entrepreneurship happens on the margins of established church institutions. New iterations of social enterprise in the church require different ways of thinking that often emerge in places of high creativity and where there is freedom to try new things. As Bickley describes, "At the heart of social innovation is a desire to not just respond to social need, but to act in ways which disrupt and change systems and markets."[3] He adds, "social innovation is more likely to occur in religious traditions that are not comfortably part of the establishment."[4] It is excellent if established institutions want to engage in redemptive entrepreneurship. They should proceed. But often long-established institutions find it difficult to engage in the radically different work that social innovation requires. This suggests that investors need to look outside their normal networks for people and organizations on the margins who are doing good work outside of the normal structures.

This was true at Pres House. When Erica and I arrived at Pres House, many, perhaps most, people in our own networks and denomination expected the effort to fail. To some extent Pres House was only given the chance to succeed because it was expected to fail. There was nothing to lose except a run-down building that had come within one meeting of being sold. So established church leaders let us play around with it. We had space and room to take risks and try new things programmatically and financially. That remains true today as Pres House exists structurally with a great deal of freedom.

Ours is what government and business entities sometimes call a "skunkworks" project. Skunkworks projects are set up outside the normal operation of an organization to give space for creativity and problem solving that will be unimpeded by the processes, structure,

lenges," Religion News Service, October 30, 2018, https://religionnews.com/2018/10/30/church-run-credit-unions-keep-the-faith-despite-challenges/.

3. Paul Bickley, *Doing Good Better: The Case for Faith-Based Social Innovation* (London: Theos, 2017), 32.

4. Bickley, *Doing Good Better*, 26.

and culture of the parent organization. Though not formally set up as a skunkworks project, Pres House thrived in large part because it was given the freedom to experiment and think very differently about how to serve college students today.

There are many redemptive entrepreneurs hard at work outside the normal established networks in churches. Perhaps they have one foot in, and one foot out of, the church world. Or perhaps they don't want to be held back by the systems and culture of churches, which may stifle innovation, and so they operate totally outside the normal church structures and networks. Just as God is at work in the world whether we participate in it or not, these innovators will keep doing their work whether church investors join them or not. But much more fruit will be born when established institutions deploy capital into innovation on the margins. And that takes effort to seek out.

As I noted earlier, many redemptive entrepreneurs struggle to access capital. Church networks that are full of relative wealth have a much easier time funding new ventures than those from lower wealth communities. While Pres House was marginal in many respects, as an organization affiliated with the Presbyterian Church, USA, we had much more ready access to commercial lending and denominational capital than other redemptive entrepreneurs who are doing equally important work. As a white, male executive director, I was able to walk into conversations with lenders and expect to be heard. Sadly, the same is often not the case for my friends who are people of color. It was not an easy process to secure our financing, but the doors were there to be opened. Church-based impact investors need to be looking beyond their own networks to see where they can open doors in more marginalized communities.

Investors seeking to truly invest in social and redemptive impact can ask themselves these questions: Who are on the front lines in our community engaging in the most innovative or effective redemptive work? How are they funded? How might their impact multiply if they received an investment of capital ten times or one hundred times the size of their current funding stream? Who knows those folks and can make introductions? How can investment be made in those people and ventures without co-opting their work or perpetuating unhealthy racial and social dynamics?

In the course of my research on this subject, I have met many incredible people doing amazing work. One of the new friends I had the privilege of making was Nikki Hoskins. Nikki is a PhD student in Christian social ethics at Drew University Divinity School. Her dissertation research focuses on Black women's eco-religious and housing activism in Chicago. She has been exploring the idea of building tiny homes on empty lots in under-developed neighborhoods in Chicago. Her interest in providing housing options for the community comes out of her own experience growing up. Nikki writes, "When my parents divorced, my family was forced to choose between living in a housing project that was located on top of a toxic waste dump (which my dad had grown up in) or to be homeless. Homelessness was the lesser of two evils. We ended up couch surfing until my mother's friend offered us a room in her small apartment. My siblings and I all lived in one room. We each had a twin-size mattress and one plastic container bin to hold all of our possessions, stationed diagonally on the floor. We lived like this throughout high school and college while my mother waited for a Section 8 voucher. For years, I laid awake asking God for a home. We didn't need a big house, just a place of our own."[5]

Her vision is for churches to acquire land or use their own land on which to put eco-friendly tiny homes. The homes, of-

5. Nikki Hoskins, "Ending Poverty through Environmentally Conscious Living," *Patheos*, November 29, 2017, https://www.patheos.com/blogs/faithforward/2017/11 /ending-poverty-environmentally-conscious-living/.

fered on a rent-to-own basis, would give families a good place to live that after seven years, they end up owning. Nikki envisions churches providing wraparound social and spiritual services for the residents of these communities.

One of the key issues Nikki is wrestling with is ownership. She is seeking to design this enterprise in such a way that ownership remains in the community and transfers to the residents. Her goal is to design the venture so that any wealth created in development doesn't just flow out of the community to developers or investors, however well-meaning they may be.

Nikki's other challenge is accessing capital to begin this project. She does not have ready access to "friends and family" capital, and the churches she is partnered with do not have many capital assets to work with. What is needed is a partner investor who is willing to provide capital to help get this started and who supports the vision of ownership and wealth remaining in the community.

### Focus on Impact First, Financial Return Second

True impact investment in the church-related ecosystem will require a shift in perspective and a reordering of the starting point for investment decision making. Traditional investment, and even socially conscious investing, begins by placing financial returns as the primary objective. Consider even a very rigorously ESG (environment, social, governance)–screened investment portfolio. It begins with the goal of generating the highest return possible at the lowest risk for the capital that is put to work in the portfolio. Screening is then done to remove the bad companies and problematic investments, but the basic investing premise remains the same.

Often this is driven by the needs of the organization to derive revenue from their investments. Endowments are expected to perform at a certain financial level. I had the opportunity to spend some time in London recently with the head of responsible investing for the church commissioners who manage the Church of England's $10 billion endowment fund. They do a very small amount of impact investing and are largely driven by a mandate from the Church of England to generate a certain financial return on investment each year. In a typical two-pocket approach, this investment income then provides funding for parishes, pastors, and other church operations. In an environment where giving from members is nowhere near enough to sustain their regular activity, these investment returns are vital for the ongoing operation of the church. This is the standard approach to investing church assets. We begin by asking: "How much money do we need, or want, to make?"

But is this the right starting point? Returning to the scriptural witness and legacy of the church, I must again ask: Is making money the primary purpose of our capital? I do not believe it is. I believe the primary purpose of church capital is to transform lives and communities. It is to have an impact. Which means that the starting point for investment should not be, How much money do we want to make? The starting point should be, *What good can our capital do in the world*? Shifting the primary question is vital. By asking this question first, we shift the purpose of capital from building more barns to being rich toward God. We shift from making money with money to making impact with money. Our end goal becomes maximizing social returns rather than maximizing financial returns. That is the essential shift we need to make in the church.

There are two key, somewhat related concepts taught in business schools that are typically applied to money that should in fact be applied to impact. The first is the "time value of money," and the second is "opportunity cost." The time value of money is the idea that money today is worth more than money in the future because money today can be invested to earn interest. So $1,000 today is worth more than $1,000 received in three years. Assuming a 5 percent return, $1,000 today will become about $1,158 three years from now.

The other concept, opportunity cost, describes the fact that if money is spent on one thing, it cannot be spent on another. This is an obvious but important idea. If a business spends money to buy new equipment, they need to consider how much more value that new equipment will create for the company versus other uses for that money, such as investing it or buying more supplies for production. On a personal level, if I spend one hundred dollars to buy movie tickets and popcorn for my family for an evening of entertainment, I must take into account the opportunity cost of not being able to take them all out for a nice meal with that same one hundred dollars. Which choice will provide the most benefit for that one hundred dollars? Each of my family members would likely argue a different answer to that question. Wherever money is spent, some other use of that money is missed: that is the opportunity cost.

Both concepts could be equally applied to social impact decisions. John Fullerton, founder of the Capital Institute and former J. P. Morgan managing director, reminds us that when it comes to social impact, "Time is not on our side. Consider the *time value of impact* as well as the time value of money." The longer we wait to address social problems, the harder those problems become to solve and the more people suffer in the meantime. It does not make sense to build bigger barns to save so much of our assets when we can use them for good that can be done right now. There is an account of a business school student asking the renowned investor Warren Buffett whether it is better to make a bunch of money as quickly as possible first to give more away later, or to give away money as you go. Buffett supposedly answered, "Isn't that a little like saving up sex for your old age?"[6] Every day that we save for future impact we miss out on impact that can be had today.

6. As recounted in Simon, *Real Impact*, 36–37.

Just as we should give heed to the time value of impact, we would do well to consider the opportunity cost of not acting with our capital now. For every moment our capital is in the hands of Jeff Bezos and Mark Zuckerberg, it is not at work for good in our communities. Our investment can only be made in one place at a time. It is either at work helping to grow Fortune 500 companies or it is at work changing lives and funding innovation. The opportunity cost of traditional, even socially screened, investing is huge. We have enormous opportunity to do good with our capital, and we are squandering that opportunity with traditional investing. It all begins by changing our primary investment question from "how much money do we want to make?" to "what good can our capital do in the world?"

Someone who understands well the opportunity cost of traditional investing is Sister Corinne Florek. Sr. Florek is a nun with an MBA and the executive director of the Religious Communities Impact Fund (RCIF). I first met Sr. Florek in her small office in Oakland, California, where she held nothing back in her skepticism of impact investors who seek market-rate financial returns while also trying to invest for impact. Sr. Florek is often invited to speak at conferences and gatherings about impact investing because she has been doing it longer than most. She ruffles some feathers in the wonderful way that prophets so often do.

Sr. Florek is serious and committed to impact first. Which for her and her fund has meant taking financial returns as low as they can get—0 percent. For twelve years RCIF has pooled investment from Catholic congregations and communities of religious women to invest in local, national, and international impact work. Sponsors to the fund receive 0 percent interest, and RCIF lends the money out at 2 percent. This keeps the cost of capital very low for borrowers and the impact of the money very high.

RCIF loans to the Community Development Finance Institutions (CDFIs), land trusts, microfinance funds, and directly to some nonprofits. They focus on providing capital to people in low-income, low-wealth communities, and supporting women and children. Sr. Florek explains why they focused on loans: "We did not want to own the assets in these communities. We wanted the local people to own these assets."[7] This decision is vital to ensuring that the real beneficiaries of impact investing are those on the ground and not the investors.

Sr. Florek explains how impact investing connects to her Catholic faith and where she sees God at work in managing money. "This is about ministry," she says. "For me, it's all about incarnation and God working through us. Our mission statement as Adrian Dominicans is that we are co-creators of justice and peace." She goes on to explain that young people are on the front lines of pushing for something deeper in life and work. "There's a lot of hunger among young people to work for something of value." She sees impact investing as one way to more fully engage young people with the work of the church.

Sr. Florek retired in 2020 but has left an indelible mark on religious impact investing. She has shown us how it can be done with integrity and with maximum focus on impact first.

## Demand Rigorous Business Plans and Excellence in Outcomes

Just because a social enterprise is primarily focused on social mission, is launched by a faith-based community, or is run as a not-for-profit doesn't mean it shouldn't be held to high standards of financial and impact performance. It does not benefit anyone to expect less of social enterprise than one would expect of a successful business. Social

7. Gail DeGeorge, "Q & A with Sr. Corinne Florek, Helping Sisters Invest to Develop Communities," *Global Sisters Report*, January 21, 2020, https://www.global sistersreport.org/news/ministry/news/q-sr-corinne-florek-helping-sisters-invest -develop-communities.

entrepreneurs must attend to their business model and ensure that it works, and investors should expect any project they are investing in will do just that.

Impact investment can in fact be more effective in driving excellence in management and outcomes than grant making. To pay back an investment with some financial return, a social enterprise must have a business model that works well enough to have some margin. The vast majority of nonprofits receiving donations and grants run their operation and programs well. But when grant and donor money doesn't have to be paid back, it is easier to run an inefficient or poor operation that slides under the radar of the grantor or donor. If the support an organization receives is in the form of investment, however, they will have to create and run an efficient and successful business operation to repay that investment with interest. Poor management or operational skill will eventually lead to an inability to pay back investors. Impact investors should not be shy about requiring repayment, asking for financial return, and demanding a rigorous business plan, for by doing so they can push a social enterprise to perform better.

This is true for us at Pres House. While I would hope that we would seek excellence in all that we do no matter what, the fact that we have to pay our bondholders and the synod back, with interest, forces us to run an efficient and effective operation. We have to provide a high-quality, high-value service for residents living in our apartment building in order to maintain full occupancy and ensure that our business model works. This reality impacts a myriad of day-to-day decisions about how we spend energy and resources, when we update and upgrade our facilities, what is expected of employees and contractors, and so on. We are constantly balancing doing the work (our mission) with making it work (the business). Our investors expect this of us, and we hold ourselves to a high standard in order to meet those expectations.

There are, of course, limits to this. There are some functions and services that cannot pay back investment or provide financial returns.

Grant money serves a vital role in catalyzing and supporting social enterprise, including at Pres House. While we run a strong social business, we also need the support of donors and grants to further advance our mission. But investors need not shy away from high expectations.

Rising to those expectations leads to good results in three areas: First, and most obviously, running a strong business means we perform well financially. We have sufficient funding for our program as well as enough to pay our investors back on time with financial returns. Everyone in the system benefits. Second, we develop financial resiliency. Rather than barely making it to the next round of grant money or getting bailed out by a last-minute donation, we have a financial model that can weather downturns and difficulties. We are not living week to week or month to month as an organization but have a robust and solid financial backbone that gives us space to plan for the future and manage ups and downs. Third, and most importantly, running a strong social business helps us carry out our mission better. As we do well attracting residents, keeping our building full, providing an excellent living experience to residents, and so on, we also do well influencing their lives with the mission outcomes we are aiming for. The two aims, business outcomes and mission outcomes, rise together.

This last point is a reminder that in addition to expecting strong financial returns, an impact investor should expect strong social impact returns as well. If the blended value of an impact investment is the combination of financial return and mission impact return, then effectiveness in both should be sought after. Good intentions are not enough. Investors in social enterprise should ask for evidence of impact and look for stories of transformation in addition to reports on financial performance. By expecting rigorous business plans and excellence in both mission and financial outcomes, investors not only will reap financial fruit but will also help their partners impact lives for good.

## Seek to Create More Value Than What Is Extracted

After flipping the primary goal and starting point from financial return to social impact, and expecting excellence in outcomes, a church-based impact investor must then consider what sort of financial return he or she is aiming for. The question that was primary in traditional investing now becomes an important secondary question: "How much money do I want/need to make?" Morgan Simon suggests that investors often skip this step because they assume the obvious answer is to "make as much money as possible, as fast as possible."[8] But we must challenge that assumption. That view of money is a social construct that needs deconstructing.[9] For the purpose of our capital is not to make as much money as fast as possible.

One of the phrases often uttered in impact investing is "Do well and do good." What this phrase suggests is that an investor can make a lot of money while at the same time having a lot of positive social impact. Sometimes this is possible. But often it is not. Financial returns on investment have to be extracted from somewhere. Facebook generates strong returns for shareholders because they extract a lot of value from us, the users of Facebook, who allow them to sell our profiles, activity, and data to advertisers for huge sums of money. Exxon Mobil provides strong returns to investors because they are literally extracting that value from the earth in the form of oil and gas.

So, how does an impact investment compete with those sorts of extractive business models? It is difficult. Some sectors can provide high returns, such as renewable energy. But social enterprises serving the working poor in Latin America or providing jobs for formerly incarcerated individuals will have a very difficult time competing with the investment returns of Facebook without unfairly extracting that revenue from the very people and communities they are seeking to serve.

---

8. Simon, *Real Impact*, 169.
9. Jed Emerson, *The Purpose of Capital: Elements of Impact, Financial Flows, and Natural Being* (San Francisco: Blended Value, 2018), 2.

Impact investments are often measured against "market-rate return." The market rate is the typical return an investor will receive for an asset class in any given sector or geographic region.[10] But is this really the basis of comparison we should be using? Market-rate returns only achieve those numbers by extracting value from somewhere. If we have shifted our perspective away from making as much money as possible, then we must also shift away from always expecting market-rate returns. Simon suggests that we instead look for "reasonable returns" that create long-term benefits for all in the system.

I serve on the board of directors for Working Capital for Community Needs (WCCN), a microfinance impact fund that lends to the working poor in Latin America. Invested money funds loans of a few hundred dollars for our end borrowers to set up small local businesses. We provide our investors a return between 0 and 4 percent, depending on the terms of the investment and the choices of the investor. WCCN cannot match the returns of other investment options without extracting that extra return from our borrowers in Latin America. Truthfully, if our investors would be willing to take even lower interest rates, we could likely have an even greater impact in the communities where we lend.

> For thirty-five years, WCCN has created access to microfinance impact funds, services, and markets to improve the lives and communities of the working poor in Latin America. In that time, we have invested a total of $125 million and reached an average of twenty-five thousand small business owners every year. WCCN empowers low-income Latin American entrepreneurs by sustaining partnerships with microfinance organizations and fair-trade coffee organizations in Nicaragua, Ecuador, El Salvador, Honduras, Guatemala, Argentina, Bolivia, Mexico, and Peru. Sixty-four percent of borrowers are women, and 61 percent live in rural areas. WCCN is a nonprofit that also raises donor money

10. Simon, *Real Impact*, 41.

to support its work. It is one of only a few funds that take retail investment from individuals at relatively low initial investment levels while still paying interest back to the investor.

WCCN started as the Wisconsin Coordinating Council on Nicaragua in 1984. It initially grew out of the Wisconsin-Nicaragua sister-state and people-to-people movements, which were encouraged by President Dwight D. Eisenhower in 1956. These movements came from Eisenhower's "faith in the great promise of people-to-people and sister city affiliations in helping build the solid structure of world peace."[11] Later, through President Kennedy's Alliance for Progress, Wisconsin became a sister state to Nicaragua, so that "through personal relations our curiosity can be fulfilled by a sense of knowledge, cynicism can give way to trust, and the warmth of human friendship can be kindled."[12] Residents of Wisconsin, many of them church members, began visiting Nicaragua as part of this sister-state relationship. During the Nicaraguan conflict of the 1980s, members of WCCN traveled to Nicaragua to support residents, serve in a peacekeeping function, and report back to the people of Wisconsin about what was happening on the ground. WCCN also served as a central network for churches and other organizations providing aid in Nicaragua.

As the war wound down in Nicaragua, WCCN made the strategic decision to shift efforts to economic development in the country. WCCN led a tour in Nicaragua in May of 1991 to explore trade and investment ties in order to help sustain long-term development in Nicaragua. On that tour they learned about community development loan funds, a successful way to promote economic development. By the summer of 1992, WCCN had

11. Liz Chilsen and Sheldon Rampton, *Friends in Deed: The Story of US–Nicaragua Sister Cities* (Madison: Wisconsin Coordinating Council on Nicaragua, 1988), 16–17.

12. Chilsen and Rampton, *Friends in Deed*, 19–20.

agreed to serve as the US "marketing representative" for a "poor people's loan fund" administered by the Nicaraguan Council of Protestant Churches, Nicaragua's largest nonprofit aid and development organization. Over time, WCCN developed its own microfinance loan fund, which still operates today.[13]

From the beginning, churches and religious institutions were instrumental in the development of the loan fund. Churches were a vital source of initial investment. A number of churches and religious institutions remain major investors in the fund today. Sisters of Saint Francis of Philadelphia explain their investment in WCCN, saying, "we have been committed to community development investing as a vital part of our mission 'to direct our corporate resources to the promotion of justice, peace, and reconciliation.'"[14] For the Presbyterian Church in Geneva, "Mission is a big part of who we are as a church, and this revolving loan fund is a great way for us to help people in Nicaragua (and other countries) help themselves."[15]

Over time, WCCN began lending in other Latin American countries and changed its name to Working Capital for Community Needs. WCCN serves the poorest of the poor and provides capital to partners, and ultimately individuals, who would not otherwise have access to capital to launch or grow their microbusinesses. As Nicaragua, and other countries that WCCN supports, deals with new political and economic struggles today, the funds lent by WCCN are a vital lifeline for communities and individuals.

13. From Summer 1992 WCCN newsletter.
14. Working Capital for Community Needs, "20 Years of Socially Responsible Investing in Their Own Words" (Madison: Working Capital for Community Needs, 2011), 16.
15. Working Capital for Community Needs, "20 Years of Socially Responsible Investing in Their Own Words," 12.

Morgan Simon proposes two helpful guidelines for those seeking to do impact investing well in her book, *Real Impact*. First, impact investment needs to add more value to a community than what it extracts, and second, it needs to balance risk and return for all parties in the system.

There is a danger in impact investing that social enterprises and investors will do more harm than good in communities by extracting wealth rather than adding it. Gentrification is a well-known example of how this happens. Property developers move into a neighborhood that has seen a decline in property value and housing stock, often over many years. They buy up property and begin to build new housing. Sometimes this is done in an intentionally exploitative manner, and sometimes it is done with the best intentions. The new development may improve living conditions. It may provide some jobs and businesses and make neighborhoods safer. New development can be a great improvement for neighborhoods in decline.

But it is very common for the wealth of the community to be extracted out of the neighborhood and into the hands, and pocketbooks, of outside developers. For who owns the land that is being developed? Who owns the new buildings that are put up and the businesses that open? And who will benefit when the value of the property increases? If the property is owned by people outside of the neighborhood, then the bulk of any wealth created by development will accrue to those people—not to the families that rent the new housing, not to the businesses that rent the storefronts, and not to the people who call the neighborhood their home but own none of it. Impact investors who helped invest in such development will receive some of the wealth of the neighborhood back in their portfolio. Even if done with the best intentions, this version of impact investing may do more harm than good.

In worst-case scenarios, investors actively benefit from exploitation even while they think they are helping. Church-related investors are not immune to this risk. In the early years of the twenty-first century, Wells Fargo created an "emerging markets unit" that specifically targeted the sale of subprime loans to African Americans through, of all places, Black churches. Wells Fargo attached itself to the influence and trust of the Black church to engage in predatory lending and extract enormous sums of money from African American citizens—just before the housing bubble burst.[16]

A specific, and rapidly growing, area of impact investment that is particularly ripe for this sort of extractive failure is the opportunity zone tax incentive. A 2017 federal tax bill created a program to incentivize real estate investment in poor neighborhoods throughout the United States. State governors can designate up to 25 percent of low-income census areas as "opportunity zones." There are now more than 8,700 opportunity zones in the United States, which contain almost 25 million people.[17] Investors are able to put huge sums of money into investment projects within these zones and receive a major tax break. The idea is to incentivize investment in neighborhoods that might otherwise be overlooked. In some cases, this process is working well.

But there is a shadow side to opportunity zone investing. In many cases investors and developers were going to build in the zones already, and the tax benefits are simply increasing the significant profit they stood to gain. And the primary beneficiaries of this incentive structure are wealthy investors, not the people who live in the communities where such development is taking place. The projects being built do not have to serve the residents of the zones they are located in. Investors can receive tax breaks by building luxury condominiums or high-end hotels just as long as they are located in an opportunity zone. In fact, some of the development is leading to exactly the

---

16. Ta-Nehisi Coates, "The Case for Reparations," *Atlantic*, June 2014, https://www.theatlantic.com/magazine/archive/2014/06/the-case-for-reparations/361631/.

17. Ayesha Rascoe, "White House Touts Help for Poor Areas—but Questions Endure over Who'll Benefit," National Public Radio, July 8, 2019, https://www.npr.org/2019/07/08/736546264/white-house-touts-help-for-poor-areas-but-questions-endure-over-wholl-benefit.

opposite outcome than the stated goal. Instead, high-end housing development is raising rents and displacing longtime residents. In other words, opportunity zone investment is sometimes fueling gentrification. Opportunity zone investing is in many cases extracting more wealth from poor communities than it is creating.

One of the ways to address the danger that impact investors will take far more than they give is to seek to balance risk and return for all in the system. The traditional investment ecosystem generally seeks to shift as much risk as possible to the entrepreneur and as much return as possible to the investor. This is no surprise if the goal of investors is to minimize risk and maximize return. But there is another way to approach this. Simon calls on impact investors to share risk and return more fairly. "Even if we have the power to demand terms that put all the risk on the enterprise, we can choose, in alignment with our overall intention of maximizing value creation for the communities we serve . . . to focus on creating terms that more fairly share risk and return." After all, "who should we try harder to protect from risk: the people with wealth, or the people without?"[18]

Praxis, a faith-based incubator for redemptive entrepreneurs, calls out "power dynamics" as one of its six "rules of life." Their rule about power reads as follows: "Instead of accumulating power to benefit ourselves or exploit others, we use it to generate possibility for those who have less access to opportunity."[19] They reference the biblical concept of gleaning, which comes from the book of Deuteronomy in the Hebrew Scriptures: "When you reap your harvest in your field and forget a sheaf in the field, you shall not go back to get it; it shall be left for the alien, the orphan, and the widow, so that the LORD your God may bless you in all your undertakings."[20] The landowner

18. Simon, *Real Impact*, 126.
19. Praxis Labs, *A Rule of Life for Redemptive Entrepreneurs* (New York: Praxis, 2018), 9.
20. Deut. 24:19.

is prohibited by the gleaning laws to reap all the profits from the land and is instead commanded to make room for others to thrive from his or her assets.

Darnell Moore, a social activist and author, talked about social entrepreneurship with Krista Tippett on her show *On Being* in August 2019. He challenged those doing community-building work to think of it as "moving ourselves out of the way and creating space for everyone—particularly those we say that we're in community with, are working on behalf of—to do the dreaming, to be the architects of their own dreams, of their own transformation, of the worlds and the communities in which they'd like to live. And then we journey along with them—never, ever commandeering the journey, which is what tends to happen."[21]

This means that investors, and enterprises, need to engage the communities they serve in all levels of "design, governance, and ownership."[22] The term "credit" comes from a Latin word that at its root means "trust." Lending, and impact investing, must be built on mutual trust between investor and entrepreneur. Communities are not simply customers or sources of labor. They must have a stake in the leadership and ownership of what is created in social enterprise. "Community is the essential form of reality," writes Parker Palmer, "the matrix of all being."[23] Walter Brueggemann suggests that "a study of money and possessions [in the Bible] makes clear that the neighborly common good is the only viable sustainable context for individual well-being."[24] And "the predatory economy of extraction"

21. Darnell Moore, "Self-Reflection and Social Evolution," interview with Krista Tippett, *On Being*, August 8, 2019, https://onbeing.org/programs/darnell-moore-self-reflection-and-social-evolution/#transcript.

22. Simon, *Real Impact*, 98.

23. Parker Palmer, *The Courage to Teach: Exploring the Inner Landscape of a Teacher's Life* (San Francisco: Jossey-Bass, 2007), 100.

24. Walter Brueggemann, *Money and Possessions* (Louisville: Westminster John Knox, 2016), xxi.

that is often part and parcel in our economic system is "countered in biblical testimony by an economy of restoration."[25]

Church-based impact investing, if done carefully to benefit all in the system, can be a tool for economic restoration. Impact investing can serve to counterbalance an economic system where the goal is to create new needs in order to sell more products. Instead of helping to create more need, impact investing can inject capital into meeting existing needs of individuals and communities. Investors can do this by seeking to create more value than they extract and by ensuring that risk and reward are shared more equitably with their partners.

## Provide Space for Risk and Failure

Risk taking and failure are essential ingredients in redemptive entrepreneurship and social innovation. By their very nature, they require trying things in new ways and experimenting. But social enterprises and entrepreneurs cannot engage in risk taking and innovation if they don't have funding partners and investors who are willing to share some of that risk. If we put two of the ingredients together—the need for space to take risks and fail, and a sharing of that risk among all parties in the system—it becomes clear that investors must be willing to accept some additional risk themselves to engage in this work well. If investors insist on eliminating as much of their risk as possible, they stifle creativity and innovation because there will be no space for redemptive entrepreneurship to experiment and thrive.

Creating space for risk taking and innovation begins by accepting that failure is part of the process and welcoming the learning that comes from failing. Shannon Hopkins, innovation expert and cofounder of RootedGood, says, "True innovation involves many failed attempts. When something doesn't work the way you plan for or imagine, it's the

25. Brueggemann, *Money and Possessions*, xx.

best opportunity for learning."[26] This is a vital orientation for redemptive entrepreneurs and social enterprises to take. It is equally important for funders and investors to take this view. If investors don't share this view, they will force innovators to avoid, or worse yet, hide, their failures in order to present the picture they think investors are looking for.

This is a vital growing edge for church institutions, as many are particularly averse to embracing risk and failure. The memory of a program or idea that failed lingers for years and years, and the failure is always brought up when something new is suggested. There is such a fear of failure that in many quarters of the church new things are almost never even tried. This is especially true if money is involved. If it is going to take money to do something, there is often an even greater fear of failure. There is an unspoken expectation that when money is granted, or new ventures launched, failure is not an option.

We need to set this fear of failure aside in the church and be willing to take some risks. After all, what is there to lose? Members? Buildings? We are well down that road already. There really is not much to lose at this point. We might as well try some new things and know that absolutely, for sure, some of those new things will fail. If nothing is failing, nothing is being tried. It is impossible to innovate without failure—in fact, failure should be encouraged because it means that risks are being taken. Investors can help set the tone for this and expect, not 100 percent success, but good efforts, thoughtful risk taking, and, yes, failure.

Practically, investors can encourage innovation and risk taking through the specific structure they establish with their investments. A redemptive entrepreneur can secure investment or borrow money from a wide variety of traditional banks and investors if they have a long track record of success, can pay money back quickly and with high returns, and have a low-risk business model. But many of the most innovative social enterprises cannot promise any of those things—at least not at first. Innovative redemptive entrepreneurship very often requires investment that can tolerate higher than normal

26. From email exchange with Shannon Hopkins on November 20, 2020.

risk with lower than normal financial returns and that doesn't need to be paid back for a long time. The details of those investment terms make the space for risk, failure, and innovation. And church-based investors are extremely well positioned to invest on terms that specifically encourage innovation and risk taking.

One simple but extremely effective way to create space for risk taking and failure is by giving redemptive entrepreneurs a long runway of time before they need to return earnings or investment capital. This is called "patient capital," capital that is willing to ride out some of the ups and downs, the trials and errors, and still stay in the game. Patient capital does not need to be paid back quickly and can wait to give more chances for experimentation before expecting to be paid back or to receive a return on investment. Where a fear of failure is often a weakness for churches, patient capital is a massive potential strength that churches have to offer the social enterprise sector.

Many traditional investors, even impact investors, are looking to place capital into service and then receive that capital back relatively quickly. They are reluctant to have their capital tied up for years. The typical venture capital model in start-up business operates on an assumption that a new business will take lots of investment early on; will scale up very quickly; will be acquired by another, larger company; and will pay the investors back with a hefty return a few years later. But this model doesn't work for many social enterprises that seek to provide impact in communities over the long term. Often social enterprises need access to capital for years.

As Ted Levinson of Beneficial Returns notes, "Social enterprises are solving some of society's biggest challenges including poverty, declining soil health and low crop yields, environmental degradation, waste and limited access to sustainable energy. However, social enterprises, particularly those operating in developing countries, struggle to secure long-term debt. This keeps many social enterprises small and unable to grow their solutions to the scale of the problems they are addressing."[27] The affordable housing project idea I proposed in chapter 8 would need capital that was patient enough for leasing to stabilize, property values to rise, and sales of some units to be completed so that the investment could be pulled back out and then put to use somewhere else. A social business that gives good jobs to formerly incarcerated individuals will need patient capital that remains in the organization long enough for them to increase sales, pay off other debts, and so on.

The good news is that the church is full of patient capital! Of all the institutions in the world that have capital that can wait a long time, the church is at the top of the list. While it is true that individual congregations are closing, as a whole, the church has no intention of going out of business. The Christian church has been around for two thousand years. We can expect some form of it to be around for at least a few more. And many church-related institutions have capital that they can make available for a long time. Many endowments and foundations have funds that they plan to invest indefinitely—funds they don't plan to spend down for a long, long time. This is perfect patient capital. This capital could be invested in social enterprises, earn a modest ongoing financial return, make a huge impact in communities, and still be there for years. Church-related impact investors can provide just the sort of patient capital that community-oriented social enterprises need to experiment and take some risks for the sake of real impact.

Financing social enterprise is often like fielding a soccer team. The game can't be played without a whole group of players. This is especially true in property development. For example, affordable housing typically requires a combination of government tax credits, bank loans (sometimes from more than one bank), community development grants, and more. They are all needed to make the project

27. From conversation with Ted Levinson.

work. And the more risky or difficult the project is, the more players are typically needed. Some of those players are willing to get in the game only if the conditions are just right. Traditional lenders, for example, need just the right mix of risk, return, and liquidity to start playing. Church-based investors can help entice them to move off the sidelines.

The team of investment players build what is called a "capital stack" of finance. This capital stack can be made up of different types of financing. For example, the base layer could be formed by donors not seeking their investment back, followed by a layer of investors seeking principal back but willing to take zero return on the investment, followed by a layer of investors seeking principal back plus a below-market-rate return, and so forth up the stack (see diagram below). Each investor or donor willing to put in money with lower expectations entices more risk-averse, or return-focused, investors to get off the sidelines and play. There are countless ways a capital stack can be designed.

When donors, foundations, or investors are willing to take disproportionate risk, or concessionary financial returns, they also create a scenario where more traditional investment is willing to get in the game as well. This is called "catalytic capital" and is a powerful spark that makes possible projects and enterprises that would otherwise not happen. Catalytic capital can be offered in all forms of financial instruments, from loans to equity positions to guarantees where no actual money changes hands but a donor or investor guarantees payment if a need arises, thus reducing the risk for the next layer of investors. Capital becomes catalytic when it makes possible something that couldn't otherwise be done.

Tideline consulting describes the five Ps of catalytic capital: price—accepting a below-market-rate return; pledge—providing a guarantee that reduces risk for other investors; position—taking a secondary or subordinated position in the financing structure; patience—accepting a longer or especially uncertain time period of investment;

and purpose—accepting nontraditional terms to meet the needs of a project (such as smaller than typical investment size).[28] Church-related investors have the opportunity and flexibility to engage in these five *P*s and provide space for risk and failure by deploying catalytic capital.

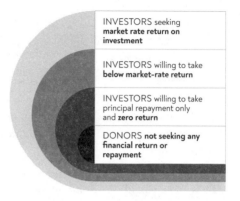

INVESTORS seeking **market rate return on investment**

INVESTORS willing to take **below market-rate return**

INVESTORS willing to take principal repayment only and **zero return**

DONORS **not seeking any financial return or repayment**

When the Synod of Lakes and Prairies made an investment at Pres House in the form of a subordinated loan, they were providing a form of catalytic capital. Pres House was unable to secure favorable financing terms from traditional commercial options due to the 2008 financial crisis. So the synod stepped in to "close the gap" and provide the capital we needed to make the whole project work. Without their investment, our financing structure would have fallen apart. Their risk, though not unreasonable, was higher. But their impact was enormous. Their $2.5 million loan made the entire $17 million financing package possible. The financing structure, and ultimately our mission to serve university students, depended upon a partner willing to provide catalytic capital.

This is a good place to note the powerful role philanthropy can play in creating space for risk and failure. The focus of this book has been on investment capital rather than on philanthropic capital. But donors and foundations also have a vital role to play on the team and in the capital stack.

28. "Catalytic Capital: Unlocking More Investment and Impact," *Tideline*, March 2019, https://tideline.com/wp-content/uploads/Tideline_Catalytic-Capital_Un locking-More-Investment-and-Impact_March-2019.pdf, 7.

One of the challenges of investing in social enterprise, especially early stage projects and businesses, is that those enterprises may fail. This, of course, puts investor capital at risk. For example, if an investor places money in ten enterprises and even one or two fail, the loss of that investment will have a significant negative impact on the overall return of the investment portfolio. Foundations or donors can dramatically reduce the risk for investors by providing philanthropic money, which becomes the first money lost if enterprises fail or cannot pay back their obligations fully. A combination of donated money with investment money becomes "blended finance" for the project or enterprise. A blend is created from investors seeking to be repaid and donors who view their contribution as a grant rather than an investment seeking to be repaid. The donor money significantly reduces the risk profile of the overall project and makes it more palatable for investors to participate. Any donated money that remains after adjusting for losses remains in play by increasing the capacity of the enterprise(s) funded or by being recycled into new projects. Program-related investments (PRIs) are a common way that foundations can deploy catalytic capital, since the tax code allows PRIs to count toward a foundation's annual distribution requirement if the capital is deployed with the foundation's charitable goals as the primary purpose and financial return is not a significant purpose.

Church-based investors can have a dramatic effect on the financing game for social enterprises and redemptive entrepreneurs. But they too must get off the sidelines and start playing. By offering an empty church building as the site for a new venture, closing a financing gap by providing a low-interest loan, or making a long-term investment in a community-based project, church-based investors can create space for risk and catalyze innovation.

# 12

## *Where Do We Go from Here?*

I remember a fad from my childhood that suddenly became all the rage—Magic Eye books. These were books filled with computer-generated images containing squiggles of colored lines and patterns that looked like nothing much. But if I stared at the images in a particular way—looking past the image on the page—then a three-dimensional shape would appear. The random colors would suddenly pop out to become a dinosaur or a mountain scene or a person reaching out a hand to touch me. When viewed correctly, what appeared to be an empty page revealed itself as something much more interesting and exciting.

I believe the current situation facing the church and church institutions is a little like a Magic Eye image. Upon first glance, it doesn't appear that much is left on the page. Years of decline, a fear of risk and failure, and a perceived lack of resources have left us thinking that there isn't much to work with. But as we look past those limits, limits we have largely placed upon ourselves, something remarkable and beautiful comes into view. We see that we are not broke but that we have enormous resources at our disposal. We see that there are different ways to put God's gifts to work in the world that can fuel innovation. We see that opening our storage barns and putting capital to work can help meet the needs of our communities, address past and current injustices in our society, and transform lives.

As I look past the limits to see where we are headed, the image that emerges in my mind's eye is a garden about to burst forth in spring. The bedrock below us is solid—built on sacred Scripture and ancient tradition that invite innovation in our practice and generosity with our money. The ground is fertile—filled with the seeds of ideas, entrepreneurs, and new ventures bursting forth with new life. And all the natural resources this garden needs to grow are available to us in the form of our property, buildings, money, and most of all, people. God is the master gardener, but we are invited to help. We have to join in the effort. We are invited to cultivate this garden so that its beauty and nourishment will feed and inspire us all.

## Cultivate the Garden

So, how do we cultivate this garden of new life? I believe if each of us engages in the following activities, we will multiply each other's efforts and encourage the new growth that is springing up all around us.

*Plant seeds by expanding imagination and sharing stories.* Often the first barrier to doing something new is to envision what the new thing could be. We need to share stories with each other about what is working and what isn't. Please share dreams with me about what could be, and I will share dreams with you. Often a well-developed story is enough to spark more hopeful and creative thinking about the use of property and assets. Stories are the seeds that grow into new ideas.

*Prepare the soil for growth through theological reflection, research, and mapping the ecosystem.* I have begun this on a limited basis in this book, but there is ample room to develop and share theological reflection around property, money, and mission in the twenty-first-century church. While remaining rooted in the historic traditions and theology of the church, some are asking new questions and experimenting with new expressions of church. Theological reflection on the roles of property and money in these new expressions of mission will add a richness to the ecosystem. This could include conversations and interaction with other fields of study such as economics and sociology.

Additional research would also help provide a deeper understanding of the needs and opportunities. Some of the questions that have begun to be answered but could be fleshed out further are the following: How many churches are expected to be closed in the next decade? Who owns those properties? How much is that property worth? Where is such property located, and what other uses might there be for it? What is the total value of church endowments in specific denominations or within a geographic area? What economic potential could networks of churches have in their communities if they put capital to work differently? What projects and practices have been successful (both financially and for mission), and what projects and practices have not worked well? Why? Further research and reflection will prepare and enrich the soil for more new growth to emerge.

*Tend the garden by providing support, community, tools, and resources for congregations, denominational bodies, pastors, and other leaders.* There is a need to develop and share tools and processes for congregations to engage in this work. The focus here begins with deep reflection on how property and money can best serve mission for a particular organization or community and then moves toward specific tools for development. This is an area my partners and I at RootedGood are working on. We are building a toolbox of resources for congregations. We are also convening cohort learning communities of congregations, practitioners, denominational leaders, and educators to journey together around their questions of property, money, and mission. They will together share information from experiments and provide mutual inspiration, imagination, and support. Seminaries and other institutions preparing new pastors, and providing continuing education for existing pastors, could include training on money and meaning to help pastors develop theological and practical skills for this work.

*Water the garden by opening the spigot of our invested assets and developing new funding and financial models to facilitate the shift of capital from dormancy to new life.* While there are many impact-investing-fund options out there that individuals, congregations, and church-related institutions can invest in today, there is an opportunity to launch new kinds of funds and financial services products that specifically meet the needs of faith-based impact investors. A particularly important consideration is how to appropriately and effectively redistribute capital from areas of the church that are overresourced (often white congregations and communities) to those that have been historically underresourced (often congregations and communities of color). Institutions that have funds available in endowments could begin experimenting with taking a portion of their invested funds out of traditional investments and putting it to work in new ways. Start with 10 percent or start with 1 percent, but start somewhere.

## Start Something Somewhere

What if you or your organization wants to get even dirtier and get to work on something specific in this emerging movement? What if you want to move from thinking, reading, or talking about this into direct action?

Do it! Start something new. Or fund something new. At the most basic level, those are the best ways to get directly involved. The chart below shows a spectrum of options for getting involved in this work along two axes: (1) engaging in redemptive entrepreneurship directly, or (2) activating capital assets to invest in others. Both are vital to support the growth of this movement.

We need people and organizations to start new social enterprises as redemptive entrepreneurs. Nikki Hoskins and her tiny-homes project in Chicago is an example of this. What ideas do you have for serving your community? What social enterprise could your organization start?

We need people and organizations to provide capital for social enterprises by engaging in impact investing or making property available for new ventures. An investment committee of a foundation moving some investments into a fund like Working Capital for Community Needs, or Arlington Presbyterian Church selling their property in Virginia to build affordable housing, is an example of this. Do you have investment assets you can pull out of companies that extract from people and the planet and instead put them in enterprises that help all of creation thrive? Is there underutilized church property in your area that could be someone's next home or place of social business?

In some cases, organizations might use their own space or money to create their own new venture, as Sacred Space did in Palo Alto by creating a coworking social enterprise in their church fellowship hall. In other cases, a congregation could play a support role in helping fund and support entrepreneurs in the community, like the Epiphany Project out of First Presbyterian Church, Atlanta. And in still other instances, all these approaches could come together from different angles, as was the case at Pres House, where we built a social enterprise, on land we owned, with an investment from another branch of our church tree. There are many different ways this work can be done.

But it will happen only if we start somewhere. If we leave things the way they are, we will continue to be disconnected from the real needs of our communities—offering a version of church that few are interested in and even fewer benefit from. If we leave things the way they are, the power of our enormous resources will continue to be put to work to develop the next feature on Facebook or speed up delivery for our next order from Amazon Prime. We can do more and better with what God has given us. Whatever approach you or your organization decides on to plant your first seedling, I encourage you to give it a try.

I started this book talking about our perception of scarcity and what we are lacking in the church. But in the end, this is a story of possibility and hope. For we have something. As we look past our fear and self-constructed limits, we see that we have an enormous abundance. We are not broke. Throughout the church in America, we have an abundance of property, buildings, investments, people, ideas, and passion. And God. We have God.

Membership and giving may have declined, but God has not declined. God's love, God's justice, God's care for all of creation is as strong as it has always been. God is at work in the world right now with all of what we have and despite all of what we perceive to be missing. And God invites us to join in planting and cultivating God's garden. There is no better time for us to dream big and take some risks. The needs are great, the opportunities, even greater. And the resources are there. We are at a moment when the church can sit on the sidelines and watch this work happening around us as we fade into the background. Or we can jump in and lead with all the theological, human, and capital resources at our disposal. Let us imagine a different future and get to work.

# Acknowledgments

Major projects like the revitalization of Pres House and the writing of this book have felt to me like cycling on a very long, spectacularly beautiful bike ride. The journey has been filled with difficult climbs, joyful descents, inspiriting vistas, and fascinating rest stops along the way. For much of the time I didn't know what was coming around the next corner or over the next rise, but I felt propelled forward mile by mile, pedal stroke by pedal stroke. But most of all, this project has felt like riding within a large, supportive peloton.

A peloton of cyclists winds its way through valleys and over hills, grouped together, riding as closely together as possible. The power of the draft is enormous. Drafting behind another cyclist can save up to 40 percent of a rider's energy. The people riding in front, to the side, and even behind a rider provide invaluable assistance. By far the easiest way to finish a long ride is to ride with a group. This is true not only while riding a bike. It is also true in life.

Completing this book has been possible only with the assistance of a huge peloton. I have benefited enormously from the draft of so many who have gone before me and ridden alongside me in these endeavors. While any errors or mistakes in this book are mine and mine alone, without a peloton of incredible people I would never have finished this book.

My experience at Pres House was instrumental in shaping my understanding of the concepts in this book. Serving as copastor and executive director at Pres House has also been one of the most challenging and wonderful experiences in my life. I have been touched by far, far too many people through my affiliation with Pres House to name everyone individually, but a few are deserving of special mention.

Erica and I would never have even heard of Pres House were it not for Randy Bare, who saw something in us that we did not see in ourselves and was instrumental in bringing us to Pres House at the beginning. I am forever grateful for his taking a chance on us and opening a door that has led to so much.

Since arriving at Pres House I have felt that I am drafting behind a powerful spirit of faithfulness and love laid down by alumni and former pastors stretching back to the very beginning in 1907. I have often stood silently in the chapel late at night wondering about what my predecessors thought and prayed about. I have had the good fortune of knowing former pastors Jim Jondrow, Melicent Huneycutt Vergeer, and Vern Visick. I have felt very strongly their spirit and that of the thousands who make up the Pres House family across the decades.

This story of Pres House, and my long and joyful tenure there, has only been possible because of past and present iterations of the board of directors, which has been made up of so many wonderful advisers, leaders, supporters, and friends. From first handing over the keys to a couple of naive twenty-somethings, to being willing to take remarkable risks, to standing together through many challenging moments, to offering thousands of hours of volunteer time and expertise, to providing space, time, and encouragement for me to write this book, the Pres House board of directors has been a steady rock throughout it all.

I cannot name all of the current and former board members who made an impact at Pres House and in my life, but a few played a particularly prominent role in aspects of the story told in this book: Tom Schwei and Craig Howard took long drives from Madison to Minneapolis with me to secure the investment from the Synod of Lakes and Prairies before any of us really knew there was such a thing as "impact investing." Bob Sorensen essentially took on a full-time volunteer job to serve as our owner representative during the construction of the Pres House Apartments. Alice Honeywell provided invaluable assistance with early fundraising efforts, government relations, and much more. Alice has also become a beloved friend of our family and offered her skilled editing expertise in the final stages of this book's development.

Alumni from before my time, and generous donors to Pres House, have served as essential supporters since the beginning of my tenure. Some took big risks to support our work well before there was any evidence that it was going to work. Many stepped forward to fill the phone lines in the state capitol, ensuring that Pres House's tax exemption remained in place. Many offered personal messages of encouragement to Erica and me, which made all the difference during times of great uncertainty and stress. This story could not have been written without their unsung support.

I have had the great privilege of working alongside a diverse and gifted staff team at Pres House over the years. Our staff team has changed in structure and makeup many times but has always been committed to serving students each and every day through ups and downs, thick and thin. I am grateful for all I have learned from each person who came on this journey. Pres House would not be where it is today without the work and commitment of incredible current and former employees.

The staff and elected leadership of the Synod of Lakes and Prairies played a vital role in this story and the thesis of this book. They pivoted from skepticism about the future of Pres House to becoming our largest investor—all for the sake of the mission. And they show us how it can be done throughout the church.

Last but not least at Pres House are the students. I cannot begin to name all the students who have changed my life and given me such joy. So I will simply say that the greatest delight in all of this work has been my relationships with students at Pres House. To say I have been impressed, inspired, and blessed by the students who have been part of the community over the years is a vast understatement. UW–Madison students are why, and how, Pres House exists.

While this story largely began for me through my work at Pres House, in recent years it has expanded dramatically. I have been blessed to connect with many incredible people doing work in the church, in impact investing, and in social entrepreneurship who have inspired and taught me. Some of these people I have known for many years and have shared hours of deep conversation with. Others were brief encounters that made an impression. All have touched me and the work that went into this book in some way. This is not an exhaustive list and I'm sure I am missing some important people, but I want to acknowledge the following individuals: Neil Ahlsten, Todd Ahlsten, Joy Anderson, Thad Austin, David Bailey, Leroy Barber, Jordan Baucum, Sadell Bradley, Rebecca Brooks, Rob Bullock, Amy Butler, Stephen Carlsen, Rudy Carrasco, Andrew Foster Connors, Mark DeVries, Patrick Duggan, Larry Duggins, Rob English, Rose Feerick, Corinne Florek, Rob Fohr, Jerome Garciano, Anna Golladay, Paul Grier, Cort Gross, Marlon Hall, Will Harris, Jon Hart, John Heinz, Katheryn Heinz, Lee Hinson-Hasty, Paul Hontz, Nikki Hoskins, Mark Hubbard, Jeff Hutcheson, Tom Jackson, Will Jacobsen, Kevin Jones, Robert Kim, Linda Kay Klein, Mihee Kim-Kort, David King, Dave Kresta, Mark Labberton, Ted Levinson, Clare Lewis, Steven Lewis, Kayoko Lyons, Craig Mattson, Chris McCain, Nancy Metzger, C. Sara Lawrence Minard, Derrick Morgan, Brandon Napoli, Katrina Ngo, Matt Overton, Min Pease, Christian Peele, James Perry, Sylvia Poniecki, Daniel Pryfogle, Mark Ramsey, Charles L. Roe, Tim Shapiro, Morgan Simon, Graham Singh, Tim Soerens, Frank Spencer, Kirsten Spira, Becca Stevens, Tony Sundermeier, Jessica Tate, Martin Trimble, Victoria White, Sidney Williams, Felipe Witchger, and Frank Yamada.

During the summer of 2017 I had the great pleasure of spending a few weeks learning about social enterprise in the United Kingdom from the following remarkable people: Paul Bickley, Daniel Brewer, Martin Clark, Tim Jones, Philip Krinks, Edward Mason, Janie Oliver, the founders and staff of HOME Café, and the community of Matryoshka Haus. I am especially grateful for connecting with Mark Sampson and Shannon Hopkins, who have since become good friends and cofounders at RootedGood. Our many thoughtful and life-giving conversations about money and meaning have shaped both this book and me as a person. Shannon and Mark played an important role in helping me refine my thinking around the alignment of money and mission, and together we created the diagram found on page 123.

I was able to meet many of these people thanks to funding and support from the Louisville Institute for a pastoral study project on church-based impact investing. I am grateful to the Louisville Institute, my fellow 2018 grant recipient cohort, and Don Richter in particular for the encouragement and support to turn my study project into a book.

A few people deserve special mention for playing an especially important role in supporting me in the effort to publish this book. This book would literally not exist were it not for the encouragement and counsel of Kenda Dean, who has been a champion of my work for years and who first suggested I write about Pres House. Greg Jones read a very early draft and opened the doors for its publication. Jed Emerson, Rosa Lee Harden, Elizabeth Lynn, and Dave Odom also read early drafts and have provided ongoing encouragement. Chris Coble, Jessicah Duckworth, and Channon Ross have provided wonderful insights, feedback, and backing across the many years that the ideas in this book were taking shape for me. Craig Dykstra not only wrote a wonderful foreword but was an early champion of my work and thoughts on this subject. And the team at Wm. B. Eerdmans Publishing Co. has been excellent to work with.

During the past few years I have had the privilege of participating in some fantastic "peloton" cohorts. I learned so much from, and had so much fun with, my colleagues in the Wisconsin Business School

Executive MBA Class of 2017. I was inspired by the remarkable gifts within my 2018–19 Convocation of Christian Leaders cohort, and they put up with me trying some of the ideas in this book out on them.

I am grateful for good friends who I can literally draft behind on my bike as we take in miles of beautiful roads around Wisconsin. Our bike rides together have kept me sane and healthy in the midst of work and writing.

I am thankful beyond measure for my family. My mother, Linda Elsdon, has been a steadfast support since the moment I was born. Thank you for always taking a genuine interest in my life at all steps along the way and for always being there for me. My father, Ron Elsdon, was one of the first authors I knew within my family. He has written not only to share valuable insights but also to further the cause of social and economic justice. I have learned much about the faithful stewardship of money from my father throughout my life. Thank you for being the first person to read this book and for your constant encouragement. My sister Anna and her spouse, Andy Domek, and their children, Claire and William, inspire me as they give of themselves professionally and personally to make our world a better place.

My work finishing this book took place during the safer-at-home period brought about by COVID-19, so I have spent a lot of time at home with my spouse, Erica, and our two daughters, Emma and Sophie. I couldn't have dreamed of a better group of women to share my daily life with. Emma and Sophie, you have been a delight to me since the moments you were born. You are now amazing young women who give me such hope for the future of our nation and planet. Your commitment to justice and love for all people is moving and powerful.

Absolutely nothing that I describe in this book could have happened without my partner in life and ministry, Erica Liu. You have been the creative force behind the ministry at Pres House. The last sixteen years spent raising our children together and pouring love and life into the community at Pres House have allowed us to share an incredible journey. We have taken turns drafting off each other throughout the years and we make a fantastic team. I am immensely grateful to live and work with you. I love you.

Finally, I give thanks to God for the abundance of gifts and joy I have experienced throughout my life. Nothing I have is mine alone—it is all on loan from God and inextricably tied up with the great peloton of people I journey with—those named here and the wider human family. Each moment of life, and each opportunity to experience something new, is a marvelous gift from God.

# *Glossary*

This limited glossary contains some of the terms used in this book and common terms one may encounter in the fields of impact investing, social enterprise, lending, etc. These terms are not necessarily defined as they would be in a business school textbook, or on Wikipedia; they are defined in a way that specifically relates them to redemptive entrepreneurship and faith-based impact investing. These are not legal definitions and should not be taken as such. Italicized terms are defined elsewhere in this glossary.

**absolute return**   In an absolute returns investing strategy, the investor seeks a specific financial return on the full portfolio of investments across a variety of investment classes (*stocks*, *bonds*, property, etc.). The absolute return required dictates and drives investment choices, sometimes without regard to the impact such investments have beyond their financial return.

**accredited investor**   A person or organization that is allowed to purchase investments that are not registered with financial authorities. Accredited investors include *high-net-worth individuals*, brokers, banks, trusts, and insurance companies. They are allowed this privileged access if they satisfy one or more requirements regarding net worth, income, governance status, or professional experience. The assumption is that accredited investors either know enough, or have enough financial means, to take higher risks on unregistered investments. Some *microfinance* and other impact investing funds only take accredited investors because the funds have not registered with regulatory bodies due to the cost and complexity of such regulatory filings.

**alpha and beta**    Measures of risk and return of a particular investment. Alpha measures the excess return on an investment relative to a benchmark investment, usually an index. For example, if a publicly traded *stock* investment provided a 10 percent return while the *S&P 500 Index* earned 5 percent during the same period, the alpha is 5. An alpha of -5 would indicate that the investment underperformed the index by 5 percent. Beta is a measure of volatility or risk of an investment or portfolio of investments in comparison to the market as a whole. For both measures, it is important to understand what benchmark is being used for comparison and why. Different types of investments provide vastly different returns, so comparing them is like comparing apples to oranges. Some investments, particularly impact investments, are more difficult to find comparison benchmarks for, as they are so unlike other investments. And social impact return is not included in the return used in alpha and beta calculations.

**amortization**    Process by which payments are made over time on a loan (principal and *interest*). An amortization schedule lays out the time line for making payments until the loan is paid off in full. Often the regular payment (monthly, quarterly, annually) is the same for each period, with a larger percentage of the payment covering interest costs and a smaller percentage paying down principal in the early part of the schedule, which arrangement is slowly shifted to the opposite over time. Thus, more of the total interest cost is paid in early years and more of the principal in later years. A standard thirty-year residential mortgage is typically set up this way.

**angel investor**    A *high-net-worth individual* who provides seed money for a start-up enterprise or entrepreneur, usually in exchange for some stake in ownership *equity* in the new venture. Sometimes an angel investor is a family member or friend of the entrepreneur. Access to significant angel investment is one of the major barriers for entrepreneurs who do not have ready connections to wealthy individuals in their family or networks.

**appreciation**    The increase in value of an asset (property, financial instrument, currency, etc.) over time. This increase may occur as a result of increased demand, decreased supply, changes in *interest* rates, or other factors. The opposite is *depreciation*, which is the decrease in value of an asset.

**asset in transition**    Property or structure in the process of being sold, repurposed, or destroyed. The thousands of church properties that are being sold or repurposed due to merger, closure, or redevelopment are examples of assets in transition.

**benefit corporation and B Corp**    A benefit corporation is a relatively new type of for-profit business entity that explicitly prioritizes positive impact on society, workers, the community, and the environment in addition to financial profit in its legally defined goals. A B Corp is similar in intent but is a specific certification of social impact given by the private entity B Labs. A benefit corporation is a legal designation. A B Corp certification can be earned by any type of corporation, including an LLC (limited liability company) or other legal form of business. The emergence of both options indicates a growing interest among stakeholders in a company's social impact and not just its financial profitability.

**blended value**    The value a business or nonprofit has based on its ability to generate financial, social, and environmental worth. Developed by *impact investing* pioneer Jed Emerson, this concept recognizes that organizations have a broader impact than simply financial performance. "Blended value" is sometimes used interchangeably with the term "*triple bottom line.*" The financial return of an investment is relatively easy to measure. The social return is much harder to quantify but is important to factor into investment decisions and performance evaluation. For example, at Pres House we pay the Synod of Lakes and Prairies a financial return on their impact investment in the form of *interest* payments. But we also provide a social return in the lives of thousands of students. Our mission outcomes, while not translated into dollars and cents in most cases, are a critical part of the blended value we provide our investors and donors.

**bond**   A *debt investment* that represents a loan made by an investor to a borrower. Bonds are used by companies, municipalities, and governments to raise money for projects and operations. Bondholders are the creditors of the issuer. A bond contains the details of the loan and its payments. Bond details include the end date when the principal of the loan is due to be paid to the bond owner; a schedule of *interest* rate payments; if the interest rate is fixed or floating; etc. In a similar way that *stocks* are bought and sold on a stock market exchange, bonds can be bought and sold individually or as part of fixed-income funds. Bonds are generally considered less risky investments than stocks, with lower financial returns; however, performance varies greatly, depending on economic conditions, the sector of investment, the specific issuer, and other factors.

**capital stack**   The finance structure of all capital invested in a project, with different levels of risk and return for different types of investments and investors. Typically, higher positions in the capital stack earn higher returns due to their higher risk. However, impact investors can provide increased impact by taking higher-risk and lower-return positions, thus providing *catalytic capital* in the capital stack. For example, the base layer of financing in a capital stack could be formed by donors not seeking money back, followed by a layer of investors seeking principal back but willing to take zero financial return on the investment, followed by a layer of investors seeking principal and *interest* back, and so on (see diagram in chap. 11).

**catalytic capital**   Investments that accept higher risk and/or lower financial returns relative to a conventional investment in order to generate positive impact and enable third-party investment that otherwise would not be possible. Catalytic capital enables or "catalyzes" investors that may not otherwise have made an investment but for the catalytic capital invested and therefore generates impact that would not otherwise have been possible. For example, a philanthropic gift or risk-tolerant investment can be used in the financing structure, or *capital stack*, of a risky venture to reduce the risk for other investors who will only invest if their risk profile is closer to that of a conventional investment. The Synod of Lakes and Prairies was willing to take a second mortgage position on their loan to Pres House, therefore assuring the commercial bank of their position and making the rest of the conventional financing possible. The project, and all its impact, could only work with their catalytic capital. Repayable grants or other forms of philanthropy are a very powerful form of catalytic capital in *social enterprise* funding.

**collateral** An asset that a lender uses as security on a loan. If the loan fails, the lender can take ownership of the collateral and try to recover some of the losses. On mortgage loans, the property serves as collateral. For example, when a home goes into foreclosure, the lender has taken ownership of the property because the borrower has not been able to keep current with the loan agreement or covenants. For *social enterprise* loans, collateral can vary from fixed assets (such as an oven for baking) to cross-guarantees from peers. Impact investors who are willing to take on higher levels of risk can offer unsecured or collateral-free loans, which may serve as *catalytic capital* for other investors who require collateral claims to underwrite their lending.

**community development financial institution (CDFI)** A private bank that seeks to reduce poverty in poorer communities through credit, financial, and other services. CDFIs focus on providing financial services to communities that are underserved by traditional banking.

**cooperative** An organization made up of individuals or businesses who have voluntarily joined together to achieve a common economic end, usually by making equal contributions into the capital required and accepting an equal share of the risks and benefits of the enterprise. Some examples of cooperatives include the following: workers who jointly own the business they work for, businesses owned by their customer members, credit unions owned by their members, and business groups that join together to make purchases at scale for lower prices.

**debt investment**   An investment based on a loan or *bond* issue. The investor lends money to an enterprise in a lump sum and then receives money back from the enterprise on an agreed-upon schedule of principal and *interest* payments (the *amortization* schedule). Or an investor may purchase bonds issued by the enterprise based on a promise to pay interest and principal over some established time horizon. Debt investments differ from *equity investments* in that the investors have no ownership stake in the enterprise. Debt investors, however, are usually paid back before equity investors if there is financial trouble for the enterprise. In social enterprise *impact investing*, setting up debt investments is often easier. However, debt obligations can leave a *social enterprise* burdened by ongoing payments requiring steady and adequate cash flow in order to meet payment schedules and adhere to agreed-upon *debt service covenants*.

**debt service covenant or contract**   An agreement a borrower makes with a lender that includes financial benchmarks the borrower must meet at all times to keep the loan in good standing. For example, a debt service covenant may require a borrower to maintain an annual income that is at least 1.2 times annual expenses (theoretically ensuring that there is always enough money to pay the lender). If the requirement is not met, the lender can recall the loan.

**default (on debt)**   Failure to meet the financial obligations on a loan or *debt service covenant* by not making scheduled payments or by violating loan covenants. A default can lead to the lender recalling the loan, seizing the collateral put up to secure the loan, or taking some other action against the borrower.

**depreciation**   (1) A decline in the value of an asset over the estimated useful life of the asset. Capital assets such as equipment are given a starting value when purchased and then depreciated on a schedule over time. (2) A decline in the value of a country's currency in comparison with a reference currency.

**diversification**    The spreading out of risk by investing in different types of investments (such as *stocks, bonds,* real estate, venture funds), different industries (technology, financial services), different sizes of companies (small cap, medium cap, large cap), different geographic locations (United States, emerging markets), or other diverse options. Diverse investments allow a portfolio to perform with more stability over time, as some investments may increase in value while others lose value. The value of all the investments in a diverse portfolio will usually not move in the same direction at the same time. *Impact investing* can be an excellent way to diversify an investment portfolio, as money is invested in *social enterprises* outside the conventional markets and may move up or down in value very differently than conventional investments. In the Pres House story, the Synod of Lakes and Prairies diversified investments from a conventional stock and bond portfolio to a social enterprise real estate project.

**divestment**    The selling of investment. In the context of social investment, divestment typically refers to the selling of a company's *stock* that is deemed problematic from an environmental, social, or governance standpoint. The investor chooses to no longer own stock in a company that the investor views as negatively impacting the world in some way. By divesting, the investor is then no longer providing capital to the company and thus no longer directly participating in the actions of the company through investment. One of the most powerful examples of divestment is how a major movement to divest from companies doing business with South Africa in the 1980s contributed to the collapse of apartheid.

**double- (or triple-) bottom-line return**    A return on investment that includes a social return (double-bottom-line) or a social return and an environmental return (triple-bottom-line) in addition to the financial return. Sometimes this is also described as returns in people, profit, and planet. I also use the idea of a triple-bottom-line return in a different way in this book. I refer to a *social enterprise* that is financed with church-owned capital as having a triple-bottom-line return when it (1) produces mission impact through the enterprise, (2) generates financial return for the enterprise and the church entity that is the investor, and (3) produces a second layer of mission impact for the investing organization when its financial returns are also used for mission and ministry. For example, the Synod of Lakes and Prairies investment in Pres House produces mission impact at Pres House, financial return for Pres House and the synod, and then more mission impact through the synod as it uses financial return for its own ministry.

**equity**    The total value of an organization's assets (what it owns) minus its total liabilities (what it owes). For *publicly traded companies*, equity also represents the amount that would be passed on to shareholders if a company's assets were all sold and after all liabilities were paid off.

**equity investment**    An investment in which an investor provides capital and takes ownership stake in the company. In start-up situations, an investor may make an early investment in a new venture in exchange for a claim on a share of the future value and profits of the venture if the start-up is successful.

**ESG (environment, social, governance) screening**    The process by which potential investments are eliminated from consideration because of questionable environmental, social, or governance activity. The acronym is sometimes used interchangeably with the more general term "socially conscious investing." Environmental criteria pertain to a company's relationship to the environment in its work, such as using renewable energy in operation, sustainable materials in products, etc. Social criteria pertain to how a company influences the people around it, such as working conditions for employees (avoiding sweatshops), company reinvestment into local communities, and social impact of business (for example, tobacco), etc. Governance criteria have to do with the corporate structures and policies such as equal pay for female employees, diversity in board and C-level leadership, etc. Companies that perform poorly against one or more criteria may be sold out of a portfolio, or the investor may engage in *shareholder activism* to try to change the company's policies. ESG screening can be done by an individual investor or, more commonly, by a fund. Many religious communities screen their investments, engage in shareholder activism to influence the companies they hold in their portfolio, and ultimately move to *divestment* from companies that consistently fail to meet established ESG criteria. There is no universal standard of screening criteria among funds or divestment lists, so individual investors are encouraged to research the criteria being used for screening before making investment decisions.

**fiduciary duty**    The responsibility a person or institution has in managing the assets of another person or institution. A fiduciary agent is expected to manage assets for the benefit of the asset owner and not in his or her personal interest. Pension funds are a classic example of a fiduciary. Fiduciary duty has often been assumed to require a fiduciary agent to aim for market-rate returns or better in investment decisions. But this guidance has been broadened in recent years to allow fiduciary agents to take *ESG* impact into account if so desired by the asset owner. Furthermore, there is a question as to whether requiring financial returns that meet relatively short-term market comparisons is really in the best long-term interest of the asset owner. See chapter 9 for more.

**financial first**    The prioritization of financial returns over social impact or *ESG* considerations in making investment decisions. Some financial-first investors may also be interested in ESG objectives, but only as a secondary concern after financial returns that match or exceed market-rate returns are met. Others may simply be seeking the highest rate of financial return possible regardless of ESG considerations.

**hedge fund**    Alternative investment fund that may use a variety of different strategies to produce a return for investors. Access is usually limited to *high-net-worth individuals* and *accredited investors* who must leave their money in the fund for at least a year. Hedge funds typically charge a high management fee of 2 percent of assets and 20 percent of profits.

**high-net-worth individual (HNWI)**  An *accredited investor* generally defined by the financial services industry as having at least $1 million in cash or liquid assets. High-net-worth individuals have access to a wider array of investment options than other investors and can often access impact investment options that others cannot.

**impact first**  Strategy of investors who prioritize positive social or environmental impact over financial return in their investments. While impact-first investors usually still look for financial return, they may be willing to accept a below-market rate of return in order to reach impact goals that are not achievable through traditional investment. I argue throughout this book that faith-based investors should always be "impact-first" investors, as our capital is best put to work invested in the lives of people and communities and not invested primarily to make more money with money.

**impact investing**  An approach to investing where money is proactively invested to produce social impact as well as financial returns. Companies and *social enterprises* receiving impact investment return this *blended value* to investors in the form of both financial returns and social and environmental impact. Impact investing is more than just negatively screening out "bad" investments that are deemed to do harm (as in *ESG* investing). And impact investing is not giving money away, as in philanthropy. Impact investing is somewhere in the middle—it is both/and. It is both an investment that generates financial return *and* an attempt to make an intentional, positive impact in the world with capital. Impact investments may produce a *market-rate* financial return alongside the social return. Or they may intentionally "give up" some financial return in order to make a larger social impact.

**initial public offering (IPO)**  *Stock* issued by a company to the general public for the purpose of raising capital. These *publicly traded shares* are highly regulated by the Securities and Exchange Commission.

**institutional investor** A company or organization that invests on behalf of other people. There are six broad types of institutional investors: endowment funds, commercial banks, *mutual funds, hedge funds,* pension funds, and insurance companies. Institutional investors typically face fewer protective regulations because it is assumed that they are more knowledgeable and better able to protect themselves and their investors. They may also qualify for lower commissions or other preferential treatment because they pool capital and invest in large amounts.

**interest** The fee charged by lenders for extending credit to a borrower, usually a percentage of the loan amount paid on a monthly or annual basis. Interest is also the financial return paid out from a financial institution to an individual or entity that deposits money in the institution, such as in a savings account. Interest rates of various types of loans and savings instruments vary depending on risk and macroeconomic conditions. Some religious communities' beliefs prohibit them from participating in traditional interest-based financial transactions, or usury.

**liquidity** Degree to which assets can be bought and sold while retaining their full value. It is often thought of as the ease with which an asset can be turned into cash. Cash is the most liquid, as it already exists in a form that can easily be transferred between parties. Large, complicated, or expensive assets like property, art, or specialized equipment are much less liquid, as they require more time and effort to buy and sell. Investments that can be sold only after a long period of time has elapsed are also considered less liquid. Investors seek liquidity in order to maximize flexibility. Some investors, including some church-related investors, invest across extended time horizons and do not need to convert all investment holdings into cash quickly. They can therefore accept lower liquidity. An alternative definition of liquidity is the ability of an institution to meet its current financial obligations, usually measured by comparing current assets against current liabilities.

**loan term** The length of time before a loan is due to be repaid in full.

**market capitalization**   The value of a company traded on the stock market, determined by multiplying the current stock price by the number of *shares* owned by all investors, also known as its outstanding shares. Market capitalization is one way of calculating the total value of a company. Companies are often denoted as large cap (large capitalization, or big companies), mid cap, and small cap.

**market-rate return**   The typical return an investor can expect to receive for a bucket of investments in a specific asset class over a certain time horizon. Investments are evaluated by comparing the financial performance of a specific investment over a certain time period with the financial performance over the same time period of a bucket of similar types of investments. For example, a single large-cap US *stock* may be compared to the *S&P 500 Index*, which is made up of large-cap companies. If it performs at a similar level, over a similar time period, it will be said to have earned "market-rate returns." In impact investing, there is a fierce debate over the merits of seeking market-rate returns on impact investments. Studies have shown that impact investments sometimes perform better than traditional investments over time, especially during downturns in the "regular" investment markets. However, I believe that while a few impact investments can achieve market-rate returns or better, true impact investment can only rarely match the returns of a typical company. This is because some amount of financial return must be given up by the investor, or shared with the wider community, in order to increase impact. Impact investors need to focus on the full *blended return* rather than just the financial return of an investment.

**microfinance**   Financial services offered to low- and moderate-income businesses or households that are underserved by traditional financial institutions. A common microfinance offering is a small loan (between $100 and $25,000) to an individual or small business. *MFIs (microfinance institutions)* also may provide bank accounts, insurance, and technical assistance to customers.

**MFI (microfinance institution)**   A financial institution that provides *microfinance* to businesses and households that are underserved by traditional financial institutions. The Grameen Bank, founded by Muhammad Yunas, is one example. It serves almost 10 million members in Bangladesh, 97 percent of whom are women.

**MRI (mission-related investment)**   An investment of assets from a foundation's endowment that seeks to create social impact as well as financial returns. Unlike a *PRI (program-related investment),* an MRI does not come from the 5 percent distribution a foundation is required to make each year but uses all or some of the 95 percent of investment capital within a foundation's endowment. An MRI must meet the fiduciary responsibility test, as it is considered an investment decision and not a grant.

**mutual fund**   A financial instrument that pools investor money and invests it collectively in *stocks, bonds,* and other assets. The investors who contribute to a mutual fund share in the gains and losses of the underlying assets that the fund has purchased. Mutual funds are managed by institutional investors. They provide an opportunity to invest without having to make decisions about which assets to purchase directly, and to diversify risk by spreading investment out among a full portfolio of assets that otherwise would be complicated or costly to purchase directly. Many mutual funds offer *ESG* options where all the assets in the fund have been screened on ESG criteria.

**opportunity cost**   The benefit an individual or organization misses out on by choosing one use of capital over another. If a business spends money to buy new equipment, that capital cannot be used to open a new location, buy more supplies for production, or some other purpose. The lost value of those other options is the opportunity cost of choosing to buy new equipment. In a similar way, when an investor chooses where to invest, there is an opportunity cost to the options that were not selected. I have expanded the concept of opportunity cost in this book to encourage the consideration of the social-impact opportunity cost of our investment decisions. Basing an investment decision purely on financial return can have a high social-impact opportunity cost.

**patient capital**   Assets an investor is willing to wait a long, or longer than normal, time to receive a financial return on. Patient capital is particularly valuable for *social enterprises* who may take a long time getting up and running and paying back investment. A typical *venture capital* structure seeks relatively quick repayment, often when a new venture is bought by an existing company. A social enterprise that exists to serve a local community is less likely to have this sort of financial "exit" strategy than a start-up business and so will need more patient capital. Church institutions that invest for the very long term are in a particularly good position to provide patient capital.

**PRI (program-related investment)**   An investment made by a charitable foundation that qualifies as a charitable expense under the tax code, allowing the foundation to include the investment as part of the 5 percent of assets it must distribute philanthropically each year to maintain its nonprofit status. The primary purpose of a PRI must be to further the stated tax-exempt purpose of the foundation. While a PRI might earn a financial return, that must not be its primary purpose. Unlike an *MRI (mission-related investment)*, there is greater latitude in the terms and returns expected of a PRI, as it is primarily considered a charitable gift and not an investment.

**private placement investment**   Also referred to as "private debt" or "private equity," this is a company *stock* or a *bond* that is offered to a preselected group of investors and not to the public. There is much less regulation of private placement investments. They are often available only to *high-net-worth individuals* and other *accredited investors*. Many impact investments are currently private placement investments. Start-up companies also often offer private placements, so they do not have to go through the much more complicated process of an *initial public offering (IPO)* to raise capital.

**publicly traded company**    A company that is owned through *shares* (*stock*) that are bought and sold freely on the open market. This contrasts with a privately held company, which is owned fully by one individual or set of partners and for which no shares are traded. Companies with shares listed for trading on the New York Stock Exchange or another exchange are publicly traded.

**redemptive entrepreneurship**    Closely related to *social enterprise*, this venture uses a business model to pursue social impact through the lens of God's work in the world. Praxis Labs defines redemptive entrepreneurship as "the work of joining God in creative restoration through sacrifice, in venture building and innovation."

**reparations**    Payments made to address a past injustice done to a person or people group. In the United States, limited reparations have been paid to Japanese Americans many years after they were imprisoned in internment camps during World War II and to some indigenous people in recognition of land that was stolen from their ancestors. Reparations have never been paid in recognition of the horrors of slavery.

**retail investor**    An individual, nonprofessional investor who invests on his or her own behalf, usually in relatively small amounts. As distinct from institutional investors who invest on behalf of others in much larger aggregate amounts, retail investors do not always have the same access to investment options, as they are protected from investing in some less regulated investments, the assumption being that they are less knowledgeable and at greater risk to invest more than they can afford. Some alternative investments, including some impact investments, are harder to access as a retail investor directly but can be purchased indirectly by investing through an institution.

**S&P (Standard & Poor's) 500 Index**    A listing of the stock values of the five hundred largest US *publicly traded companies* weighted by the relative size, or *market capitalization*, of each company in the index (higher-valued companies receive more weight). The S&P 500 Index is often quoted as an overall indication of the movement of the stock market in general, although many *stocks* that may perform differently are not included in the index. Impact investments and any *private placement investments* are not included in the S&P 500 Index.

**shareholder activism**    Action that an investor takes to exercise rights as a partial owner in a company, or shareholder, in order to influence the policy or direction of the company, often on *ESG* criteria. Actions may include correspondence, dialogue, voting shareholder proxies, and filing shareholder resolutions. For example, the Presbyterian Church, USA, has a Committee on Mission Responsibility through Investment that seeks to influence companies that the denomination invests in. This committee engages in activism around the following priorities: pursuit of peace; racial, social, and economic justice; environmental responsibility; and securing women's rights. Typically, the more *shares* an investor holds (such as an *institutional investor*, like a denomination), the more influence the investor will have.

**social enterprise**    A venture that seeks to engage in social impact while also generating revenue from operations (*double- or triple-bottom-line return*). A social enterprise may be structured as a for-profit or a not-for-profit and may or may not receive grants or donations in addition to revenue generated from operations. A social entrepreneur is one who engages in that work. At Pres House, the revenue-generating apartment community that serves students' spiritual, emotional, and intellectual needs is a social enterprise.

**social impact bond**    A contract with the public sector or government authority that pays out a return to the investor if a social outcome is met. A social impact bond is not actually a *bond*, because repayment and return on investment are only paid if social outcomes are achieved; investors receive nothing if outcomes are not met. One of the first social impact bonds was issued by a prison in the United Kingdom that raised money by promising repayment and return to investors if the relapse rate of its prisoners was lower than that of a control group of prisoners from other prisons.

**social innovation**   The use of new and creative approaches to programming, business, or social services in order to make good in the world and help people thrive. For example, Pres House built upon a social innovation of promoting the spiritual, emotional, and intellectual needs of college students through a residential living community that benefits them and that they will also pay for.

**SRI (socially responsible investing)**   Investing that takes social impact into consideration in investment decisions. Often used interchangeably with *ESG* investing. SRI primarily employs screening out companies that are deemed not socially responsible (such as tobacco producers, weapons manufacturers, etc.), based on criteria chosen by the investor or fund manager.

**stock/share**   A financial instrument that represents a portion of ownership in a company. Such ownership includes a percentage of the company's net assets and future earnings. For example, if a company has one million total outstanding shares and an individual owns ten thousand shares, that investor owns 1 percent of the company.

**sustainable development**   Development, growth, and resource utilization that consider the needs of future generations. Places high importance on preserving the sustainability of the environment so that natural assets will be available for future development and growth.

**sustainable development goals (SDGs)**   A set of seventeen goals put forward by the United Nations as a "blueprint to achieve a better and more sustainable future for all." The goals include outcomes such as no poverty, zero hunger, gender equality, clean water, clean energy, and more. The UN calls for these goals to be achieved by 2030. Many *social enterprises* and impact investors specifically target achieving these goals in their operations and investment decisions.

**time value of money (TVM)**   The idea that money today is worth more than money in the future because it can make money over time through financial returns on investment. For example, $1,000 today is worth more than $1,000 received in three years. Assuming a 5 percent return, $1,000 today will become about $1,158 three years from now.

Investors interested in social impact returns must also consider the time value of impact: that is, impact generated today with investment capital is worth more than impact generated in the future. Helping improve people's lives today is more valuable than the theoretical possibility of improving lives in the future. And many of the problems we seek to address only worsen over time, so solving problems today can have a multiplicative positive impact in the future.

**tranche**   A series of payments, or investments, made over time based on certain performance metrics being met. Comes from the French word meaning "slice." Often used by *venture capital* investors who will offer a portion of investment, a tranche, up front, with the rest to come later if the enterprise meets certain performance objectives.

**"two pocket" philosophy**   The idea, often attributed to Bill Gates, that there are philosophically two entirely separate pools of money an individual, family, or institution manages. One pocket is the money-making side. Most activity happens in this first pocket through business activity, investment for financial return, etc. The second pocket is a small pool of money where charitable or philanthropic giving takes place. Traditional investors keep the two pockets completely separate—never mixing money that is for income with money that is for charitable impact. This two-pocket philosophy assumes that activity in the much larger business and investing pocket is not connected to social impact. Impact investing brings those two pockets of money together in a unified and mission-aligned whole. In impact investing and social business all money is treated as having impact, and social impact is evaluated alongside financial returns in making decisions from one single pocket.

**venture capital (VC)**   *Equity investment,* usually made by a *high-net-worth individual* or VC fund, in early-stage companies or entrepreneurs. Typically, the funder provides investment in exchange for an ownership stake in the business. Financial investment may be accompanied by technical or other assistance for the new venture.

Venture capital is typically offered to businesses with high growth potential. In exchange for high risk (many VC-funded businesses fail and pay little to nothing back to initial investors), VC investors seek high returns and relatively quick return of capital on their initial investment. VC investment is often paid off when a new venture is bought by an existing company, "goes public" with an *initial public offering*, or receives later rounds of investment. For example, a VC investor may invest in ten businesses expecting eight to fail, one to pay back just the initial investment, and one to take off and pay back thirty times the investment or more (sometimes called a "unicorn"). Venture capital investment takes risks in investing in new ventures that traditional investors are not willing to take. However, the typical venture capital model may not work particularly well for *social enterprises* that have no "exit strategy" to sell their venture or scale up quickly enough to provide huge financial returns. Many social enterprises, while aiming to be profitable, seek long-term social impact in a community and therefore need a different investment structure and more *patient capital.*

**venture philanthropy**   Philanthropy in which large "investment" is made in experimental approaches to solving social problems. The term was originally coined by John D. Rockefeller III in 1969, who described it as "an adventurous approach to funding unpopular social causes." Venture philanthropists, like Bill and Melinda Gates, are often very active in the causes and organizations they fund by providing expertise and technical assistance.

**waterfall payment method**   A repayment approach where higher-tiered creditors receive *interest* and principal payments while lower-tiered creditors receive only interest payments. When the higher-tiered creditors have received all interest and principal payments in full, the next tier of creditors begins to receive principal payments along with their interest. Called a waterfall payment because it is structured as a series of buckets arranged in a hierarchy where the second bucket receives principal back only after the first bucket is full (paid off), and so on down the waterfall. This approach allows a creditor to pay down more expensive or term-limited debt first before moving on to lower-cost or more flexible debt. Waterfall payments may be used when building a *capital stack* of investment.

# Discussion Questions

Talking about money is difficult. In many settings talking about money, especially our own money, is even more difficult than talking about sex or politics or religion. But our relationship with money is a central aspect of faith and so it is important that we discuss it with one another. Some of the questions in this discussion guide invite you to share honestly and openly about your personal finances and your personal views on money. This may be uncomfortable or difficult for you or others in a discussion group. You may want to establish some group discussion guidelines before you begin in order to create a safe space for these conversations. Here is one suggestion for a set of guidelines to guide your discussions:

## RESPECT Guidelines for Small Groups[1]

R     take **RESPONSIBILITY** for what we say and feel without blaming others

E     **EMPATHETIC** listening

S     be **SENSITIVE** to differences in communication styles

---

1. Adapted from guidelines found in Kaleidoscope Institute, *KI Report*, https://
static1.squarespace.com/static/5c3631609772ae2563852818/t/5d2780613d10f200016
344d8/1562869859015/KI+Toolbox+-+English+PDF.pdf, 3.

| P | **PONDER** what we hear and feel before we speak |
|---|---|
| E | **EXAMINE** our own assumptions and perceptions |
| C | keep **CONFIDENTIALITY** within the group |
| T | **TOLERATE** ambiguity |

## Preface

1. What worries have you heard expressed in your context or congregation? Are any of the worries described in the opening page of the book familiar to you?

2. In what ways do you feel "broke" or limited in your resources? What do you wish you could do in your congregation or organization if there were just more money, people, or time available?

## Introduction: We Aren't Broke

1. What sticks out to you as hopeful in the story of Pres House?

2. Name and describe three complex or "wicked" problems that your community is currently facing.

3. Describe a way in which your congregation or organization has served the needs of your community beyond traditional church activities such as Sunday morning worship, Sunday School, etc.

## Chapter 1: Uncovering Abundance

1. What is one unexpected or unusual asset that your congregation or organization has that could be used to further your mission and ministry? Try to think of something overlooked or consider how a common resource could be used in a new way.

2.  The story of Pres House and examples of coffee shops, coworking spaces, day care centers, grocery co-ops, and others are some of the ways that churches are engaging in social enterprise. What other examples of church-based enterprises have you heard about or can you think of that address "wicked" problems in our world? (You will find additional examples throughout other chapters of this book.)

3.  Grants or donations *and* investments are all sources of funding that can fuel social innovation and ministry. Talk about how investment differs from donor funding. What are some of the potential benefits of investment capital for funding mission and ministry? What might be some challenges with that type of funding?

4.  Elsdon writes: "In many parts of the wider big C 'Church,' we have a lot of assets. A lot of capital. Incredibly valuable property in A-plus locations. Buildings. And massive endowments. We are not broke. In fact, the member organizations of the Interfaith Center on Corporate Responsibility (ICCR) have more than $400 billion of invested assets under management (that is billion, with a *b*)." Does that number, $400 billion in church-owned invested assets, surprise you? How does thinking about the wealth of investment money and property that churches own around the United States change the way you think about scarcity or abundance?

5.  Read Matthew 25:14–30, the parable of the talents. Then consider this scenario: Someone wants to invest $1 million in a social enterprise in your context. They want the money back in ten years and would like to be paid a small financial return each year between now and then (this is not a grant or donation). What would you do with such an investment? (Keep this question in mind as you continue to read and discuss, and return to this one throughout your conversations.)

## Chapter 2: The Way We've Always Done It

1.  As Elsdon notes, the Lake Institute for Faith and Giving has found that "81 percent of congregational revenue comes from individual donations, and 78 percent of that giving occurs during worship services, or in other words 'passing the plate' either literally or via online giving." Where does the majority of your congregation's or organization's revenue come from?

2.  Bill Gates and others have referred to a "two-pocket" approach to money where the purpose of investing is to make money and the way to solve social problems is to give money away, but the two pockets should remain separate. Impact investing breaks down that bifurcation and uses investment to address social issues. Discuss the pros and cons of a "two-pocket" approach to investing. What do you think the purpose of investment is? What are some alternatives to the "two-pocket" approach?

3.  Investing for maximum financial return and separating investment from social impact is the "way we've always done it." Why do you think that is?

## Chapter 3: Highest and Best Use—Bigger Barns or Something Else?

1.  What were you taught about money as you were growing up? What explicit and implicit messages did you receive about money from your family, church, and culture around you?

2.  Reread the parable of the rich fool (Luke 12:13–21).

3.  Why does God call the man in this story a "fool"? What is foolish about his behavior?

4.  How might this parable relate to saving for the future?

5.  How do you define abundance?

6.  What points do you think Jesus was trying to make in sharing this parable?

7. In what ways has your "land" produced abundantly (or not)? What impact has that had on the trajectory of your life and where you find yourself today?

## Chapter 4: Open the Barns, Don't Build More

1. What are some of the implications of the idea "God owns. Humans just possess for the time being"?

2. How often do you think about money in your daily life? How much influence does money have in your day-to-day decision making?

3. How much money is "enough"? How much is enough in your personal life? How much is enough for your congregation or organization? Do you feel as though you have enough? Why or why not?

4. Elsdon invites the reader to wrestle the myth of scarcity to the ground, a myth that traps us in fear and greed. How would setting aside the lie of scarcity change the way you live? What would freedom from fear and greed look like for you? How about for your congregation or organization?

5. What is the primary purpose of church-"owned" capital and money? In what ways is that purpose being fulfilled well in your context? How could your congregation or organization better align the way money is used with its primary purpose?

## Chapter 5: All Investment Has Impact—What Is Ours?

1. Think about your personal money, your institution's money, or an institution you know: Where and how is that money saved or invested? What is that money doing right now as you have this discussion? Who has access to it? Who is using it? (If you want to go deeper with this topic, do some research on where your bank

invests the money you deposit and what companies you may own in stock or bond investments. What do you find? Where is your money "spending the night"?)

2. What factors do you consider when making investment decisions with personal and/or organization money?

3. Does the impact of how your money makes money align with your values as an individual or organization? If not, what changes would you need to make to bring your investments into closer alignment with your values?

## Chapter 6: Creating a New Future by Repairing the Past

1. Elsdon writes, "The legacy of slavery and stolen land is embedded in the very fabric of our economic system in the United States. Much of the wealth of our nation has roots in money made on the backs of enslaved people on land taken from Native Americans. And church institutions are just as bound up in this reality as are any other institutions." What are some of the implications of this reality? How can today's choices about the use of capital serve to perpetuate, or begin to repair, injustices embedded in our economic system and society?

2. How is your wealth (or lack of wealth) tied up in past or current systemic injustice? Have you benefitted from, or been harmed by, injustice? Or both? What would need to change to restore justice in those areas of your life?

3. Consider these same questions for your congregation or organization.

4. If you want to go deeper with this topic, do some research on where any family wealth that might exist in generations before you came from and/or where your church/seminary/denomination/etc. derived its current assets and property from. Did any of

that wealth come from activities related to slavery? Who were the original inhabitants of the land your organization sits on and what were the circumstances that led to their leaving? What happened to those original inhabitants?

5. Elsdon suggests that investment decisions, particularly moving investment capital into intentional impact, has potential to serve as a form of reparations for the sin of slavery. Discuss this idea. How can you and your organization be involved in such a movement?

## Chapter 7: Reimagining Assets—a Higher and Better Use?

1. What is one of the most creative or meaningful social innovations you have seen happen in the church (present or past)?

2. The beloved children's television star Mr. Rogers said: "It's so very hard, receiving. When you give something, you're in much greater control. But when you receive something, you're so vulnerable. I think the greatest gift you can ever give is an honest receiving of what a person has to offer." Discuss this idea. Why is it often much harder to receive than give? How does that difficulty sometimes lead to perpetuating a separation between people, or to patronizing charity, rather than real, lasting change?

3. Reread the opening story of the introduction about Peter, the student in addiction recovery who found healing through living at Pres House. How did the social enterprise of Pres House Apartments impact his life in a way that a traditional church "program" may not have been able to? What is distinctive about social enterprise that has the potential to positively impact lives, communities, and the founding organization?

4. If you were to start a social enterprise in your context, what might it be? Could a social enterprise in your context address any of the "wicked" problems facing your community?

## Chapter 8: So Much Property!

1. Are there underutilized properties in your community? Where? What kinds of properties are they? What are the current plans for those properties? Are any of those properties owned by churches?
2. Return to your list of "wicked" problems you identified in the introduction. How might church-owned property be used differently to address those problems? What could you imagine happening?
3. Elsdon describes the difference a $1 million investment can make versus a $50,000 donation. Discuss this idea. Why is that? Is that always the case? What sorts of problems would be better solved with a donation rather than an investment?

## Chapter 9: Barriers That Hold Us Back

1. Why do you think so little impact investing and social enterprise is being done in the church? What is holding us back? What is holding you back?
2. Review the six barriers that Elsdon describes in this chapter. Which ones apply to you the most? Pick one barrier that you can work to overcome and identify three steps you will take to overcome it.
3. What do the terms "faith-based investing" or "Christian social enterprise" mean to you? What would make investing or social enterprise uniquely "faith-based" or "Christian" and how would you describe those activities? Discuss the perils of using that language that Elsdon raises toward the end of chapter 9. How can religious communities engage in this work without further splintering and dividing people from one another?

*Discussion Questions*

## Chapter 10: Ingredients to Make It Work for Redemptive Entrepreneurs and Social Enterprises

1. Elsdon writes that staying focused on core mission is like riding a bike: You must know where you want to go and stay focused on that path. Discuss that analogy. If that analogy doesn't resonate with you, what is a different analogy that helps you think about staying focused on core mission? How do you stay focused on core mission while remaining flexible and adaptive to changing times and circumstances? What traditions, practices, scripture passages, or other resources help keep you grounded and focused?

2. What is the difference between "out*puts*" and "out*comes*"? Do you measure either in your context? Identify one outcome you want to see in your congregation or community twelve months from now. How can you measure that outcome to be sure you attained it?

3. Elsdon writes, "If we don't attend to the 'business' of mission, our mission will not be effective." How does that apply to your congregation or organization? What aspects of the "business" of your mission are in need of some attention so that you can better fulfill that mission?

4. Identify the top three sources of revenue for your organization (donations, program services, rental income, etc.). If you are able, ask for or look up how much each of those sources generates and what percentage that is of your income. Is your model working to provide enough income to fulfill your mission? If not, is there one source of income you could increase upon by getting better at "raising" that sort of money? Or would it be more effective to diversify into a new source of income? Has anything in this book so far given you new ideas of how to fund your mission and ministry?

5. Make a copy of the Mission and Money map for each person in

your group. Identify five to seven of your core activities and spend a few minutes placing them on the chart based on their mission impact and financial viability. Be honest about where they fall. Discuss what you notice from this exercise. Is there anything you would like to change having seen how your activities line up on these criteria? What steps can you take to shift more activities into the black boxes on the map?

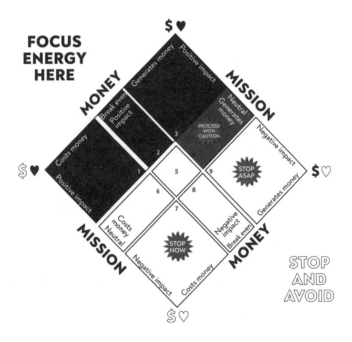

6.  Think back to first learning to ride a bike or teaching a child/ grandchild to ride a bike. What was hard about it? Discuss how that analogy relates to your current context. Does a fear of failing prevent your congregation or organization from "letting go of the brakes"? If not, proceed! If it does, where do those fears come up most? How can you cultivate an increased tolerance for risk and an embrace of experimentation in your context?

## Chapter 11: Ingredients to Make It Work for Investors

1. Where are you connected to invested assets in your life? Does your congregation or organization hold investments? Are you part of a retirement or pension fund? Do you support a charity that has investments? Does the business or nonprofit you work for have investments? Make a quick list of all the places the people in your discussion group are connected to invested assets. Highlight those that are church-related.

2. Consider these questions that Elsdon asks in chapter 11: "Who are on the front lines in your community engaging in the most innovative or effective redemptive work? How are they funded? How might their impact multiply if they received an investment of capital ten times or one hundred times the size of their current funding stream? Who knows those folks and can make introductions? How can investment be made in those people and ventures without co-opting their work or perpetuating unhealthy racial and social dynamics?"

3. Elsdon writes, "The starting point for investment should not be, How much money do we want to make? The starting point should be, *What good can our capital do in the world?*" Pick one of the connection points to investment that you identified in question #1 and then discuss what good that investment capital could do in the world. What can you or your group do to shift that capital, so it is accomplishing more good in the world?

4. How does demanding rigorous business plans and excellence in outcomes as an investor help the enterprise you are investing in? What are some potential pitfalls of making demands that are too onerous, especially in the social enterprise space?

5. Impact investors often say that you can "do well and do good" when talking about investing. What do you think of that phrase? Is it possible to do well and do good at the same time? Does one trade off against the other? In what ways?

6. Elsdon suggests that there is a risk that even well-meaning impact investors can do more harm than good by extracting wealth from communities even while trying to help them. How can you protect against that possibility in your investment decisions? How can church-based impact investors make investments in such a way as to address inequality and injustice rather than perpetuating it?

7. Do you have connections or access to "catalytic" capital? If so, how can you help put it to work to encourage experimentation and appropriate risk taking?

## Chapter 12: Where Do We Go from Here?

1. How have the examples, stories, and ideas in this book helped you see new possibilities? If you felt "broke" at the beginning, how has that feeling changed?

2. Elsdon makes an invitation at the close of the book: "Membership and giving may have declined, but God has not declined. God's love, God's justice, God's care for all of creation is as strong as it has always been. God is at work in the world right now with all of what we have and despite all of what we perceive to be missing. And God invites us to join in planting and cultivating God's garden. There is no better time for us to dream big and take some risks. The needs are great, the opportunities, even greater. And the resources are there. We are at a moment when the church can sit on the sidelines and watch this work happening around us as we fade into the background. Or we can jump in and lead with all the theological, human, and capital resources at our disposal. Let us imagine a different future and get to work.

Where do you see yourself contributing to this movement? Review the chart on page 164. Put yourself and your organization on the map. How can you get started? Could you launch a social enterprise at your church? Invest in a social entrepreneur in your community? Move endowment funds from Facebook and Google into impact investing? Open up your building for a social entrepreneur to start his or her enterprise? Or something else? Pick a way to get involved and get started. Then identify what steps you need to take to make that happen.

# Bibliography

Applewhite, Daniel. "Founders and Venture Capital: Racism Is Costing Us Billions." *Forbes*, February 15, 2018. https://www.forbes.com /sites/forbesnonprofitcouncil/2018/02/15/founders-and-ven ture-capital-racism-is-costing-us-billions/#3390ef4b2e4a.

Austin, Thad. "Social Entrepreneurship among Protestant American Congregations: The Role, Theology, Motivations, and Experiences of Lay and Clergy Leadership." PhD diss., Indiana University, 2019.

Badger, Emily. "Whites Have Huge Wealth Edge over Blacks (but Don't Know It)." *New York Times*, September 18, 2017. https://www.ny times.com/interactive/2017/09/18/upshot/black-white-wealth -gap-perceptions.html.

Balkin, Jeremy. *Investing with Impact: Why Finance Is a Force for Good.* New York: Bibliomotion, 2015.

Barnett, Susan. "The PCUSA Clerk's Annual Questionnaire 2017: Faith Based Investing." Presbyterian Church, USA Research Services, March 2018.

Battilana, Julie, Matthew Lee, John Walker, and Cheryl Dorsey. "In Search of the Hybrid Ideal." *Stanford Social Innovation Review*, Summer 2012. https://ssir.org/articles/entry/in_search_of_the _hybrid_ideal#.

Beneficial Returns. *2018 Impact Report.* http://www.beneficialreturns .com/uploads/7/5/2/0/75208167/2018_beneficial_returns _impact_report.pdf.

Bickley, Paul. *Doing Good Better: The Case for Faith-Based Social Innovation.* London: Theos, 2017.

Blank, Rebecca, and William McGurn. *Is the Market Moral? A Dialogue on Religion, Economics, and Justice.* Washington, DC: Brookings Institution Press, 2004.

Bouri, Amit. "GIIN: Why Impact Investing Is a Natural Fit for Faith-Based Investors." *Financial Advisor,* August 12, 2019. https://www .fa-mag.com/news/faith-in-finance--why-impact-investing-is-a -natural-fit-for-faith-based-investors-51034.html.

Brueggemann, Walter. *Money and Possessions.* Louisville: Westminster John Knox, 2016.

Carlson, Richard P. "Feasting on the Word—Year C, Volume 3: Pentecost and Season after Pentecost 1 (Propers 3–16)." In *Feasting on the Word: Preaching the Revised Common Lectionary.* Louisville: Westminster John Knox, 2010.

"Catalytic Capital: Unlocking More Investment and Impact." *Tideline,* March 2019. https://tideline.com/wp-content/uploads/Tideline _Catalytic-Capital_Unlocking-More-Investment-and-Impact _March-2019.pdf.

Centers for Disease Control. "Economic Trends in Tobacco." Last reviewed May 18, 2020. https://www.cdc.gov/tobacco/data_sta tistics/fact_sheets/economics/econ_facts/index.htm.

Charity Navigator Giving Statistics. Accessed July 13, 2020. https://www .charitynavigator.org/index.cfm?bay=content.view&cpid=42.

Chilsen, Liz, and Sheldon Rampton. *Friends in Deed: The Story of US–Nicaragua Sister Cities.* Madison: Wisconsin Coordinating Council on Nicaragua, 1988.

Claiborne, Shane. "A Radical Redistribution of Love." *KolbeTimes,* April 11, 2019. https://www.kolbetimes.com/radical-redistribu tion-of-love/.

Coates, Ta-Nehisi. "The Case for Reparations." *Atlantic,* June 2014. https://www.theatlantic.com/magazine/archive/2014/06/the -case-for-reparations/361631/.

Collins, Chuck, and Josh Hoxie. "Billionaire Bonanza." *Inequality.org*. 2017. https://inequality.org/wp-content/uploads/2017/11/BIL LIONAIRE-BONANZA-2017-Embargoed.pdf.

Desmond, Matthew. "In Order to Understand the Brutality of American Capitalism, You Have to Start on the Plantation." *New York Times Magazine*, August 18, 2019. https://www.nytimes.com/interac tive/2019/08/14/magazine/1619-america-slavery.html.

Dodd, Patton. "Cities Need Housing. Churches have property. Can they work something out?" *Washington Post*, November 5, 2019. https://www.washingtonpost.com/religion/2019/11/05/cities -need-housing-churches-have-property-can-they-work-some thing-out/.

Echoing Green. "State of Social Entrepreneurship 2020." Echoing Green, March 30, 2020. https://echoinggreen.org/news/state-of-social -entrepreneurship-2020/.

Einstein, Albert. Letter to his son Edward, February 5, 1930. In *Words to Ride By: Thoughts on Bicycling*, by Michael Carabetta. San Francisco: Chronicle Books, 2017.

Elsdon, Ron, ed. *Business Behaving Well: Social Responsibility, from Learning to Doing*. Dulles, VA: Potomac Books, 2013.

Emerson, Jed. *The Purpose of Capital: Elements of Impact, Financial Flows, and Natural Being*. San Francisco: Blended Value, 2018.

Ferral, Katelyn. "Church-Run Credit Unions Keep the Faith Despite Challenges." Religion News Service, October 30, 2018. https:// religionnews.com/2018/10/30/church-run-credit-unions-keep -the-faith-despite-challenges/.

Fullerton, John. "A 'Gospel of Wealth' for the 21st Century." In *Slow Investing*, edited by John Bloom. Phoenixville, PA: Lilipoh Publishing, 2011.

Global Impact Investing Network. "Engaging Faith-Based Investors in Impact Investing." *Global Impact Investing Network Report*, January 2020. https://thegiin.org/assets/Engaging%20Faith-Based %20Investors%20in%20Impact%20Investing_FINAL.pdf.

———. "Faith Based Impact Investing: Growing the Field; Global Impact Investing Network Webinar." Global Impact Investing Network. December 18, 2019. https://www.youtube.com/watch?v=yvofIxMQqMk&feature=youtu.be.

———. "2019 Annual Impact Investor Survey." https://thegiin.org/assets/GIIN_2019%20Annual%20Impact%20Investor%20Survey_webfile.pdf.

Goldmark, Alex. "Social Impact Investing: It's Not Wall Street as Usual." *Good*, October 21, 2011. https://www.good.is/articles/social-impact-investing-it-s-not-wall-street-as-usual.

Gould, Elise. "U.S. Lags behind Peer Countries in Mobility." *Economic Policy Institute*, October 10, 2012. https://www.epi.org/publication/usa-lags-peer-countries-mobility/.

Harari, Yuval Noah. *Sapiens: A Brief History of Humankind.* New York: Harper Perennial, 2015.

Hoskins, Nikki. "Ending Poverty through Environmentally Conscious Living." *Patheos*, November 29, 2017. https://www.patheos.com/blogs/faithforward/2017/11/ending-poverty-environmentally-conscious-living/.

Hout, Michael. "Americans' Occupational Status Reflects the Status of Both of Their Parents." *Proceedings of the National Academy of Sciences* 115, no. 38 (September 18, 2018): 9527–32. https://doi.org/10.1073/pnas.1802508115.

Hudnut-Beumler, James. *In Pursuit of the Almighty's Dollar: A History of Money and American Protestantism.* Chapel Hill: University of North Carolina Press, 2007.

Internal Revenue Service. "Retirement Plan Fiduciary Responsibilities." Last updated December 20, 2019. https://www.irs.gov/retirement-plans/retirement-plan-fiduciary-responsibilities.

Janus, Kathleen Kelly. *Social Startup Success: How the Best Nonprofits Launch, Scale Up, and Make a Difference.* New York: De Capo Lifelong Books, 2017.

Johnson, Todd. "Welcome to iPAR." *Medium*, March 22, 2019. https://medium.com/@todd_94277/welcome-to-ipar-b84227525f9d.

Jones, Kevin. "How SOCAP Changed 'Two Pocket Thinking.'" *Transform*, July 8, 2019. https://thetransformseries.net/2019/07/08/how-socap-changed-two-pocket-thinking/.

Jones, L. Gregory. *Christian Social Innovation*. Nashville: Abingdon, 2016.

J. P. Morgan Chase Global Research. "Impact Investments: An Emerging Asset Class." November 29, 2010. https://thegiin.org/assets/documents/Impact%20Investments%20an%20Emerging%20Asset%20Class2.pdf.

Kahneman, Daniel, and Angus Deaton. "High Income Improves Evaluation of Life but Not Emotional Well-being." *Proceedings of the National Academy of Sciences* 107, no. 38 (September 21, 2010).

Kapadia, Reshma. "How the World's Largest Pension Manager Is Trying to Make ESG Investing More Popular." *Barron's*, April 12, 2019. https://www.barrons.com/articles/pension-manager-esg-impact-investing-51555020782/.

Lake Institute on Faith and Giving. "The National Study of Congregations' Economic Practices." Indiana University Lilly Family School of Philanthropy, 2019. https://www.nscep.org/wp-content/uploads/2019/09/Lake_NSCEP_09162019-F-LR.pdf.

Laskas, Jeanne Marie. "The Mister Rogers No One Saw." *New York Times*, November 21, 2019. https://www.nytimes.com/2019/11/19/magazine/mr-rogers.html?fbclid=IwAR1M-HZvqdsDTHNp5iWOt t5HF8y-67RtFQ8VoEvwgGPstxkiPp2jzAkhBEw.

Lumley, Tris. "Raising the Bar on Nonprofit Impact Measurement." *Stanford Social Innovation Review*, July 10, 2013. https://ssir.org/articles/entry/raising_the_bar_on_nonprofits_impact_measurement.

Mather, Michael. *Having Nothing, Possessing Everything: Finding Abundant Communities in Unexpected Places*. Grand Rapids: Eerdmans, 2018.

Miles, Tiya. "1619 Project: How Slavery Made Wall Street." *New York*

*Times Magazine*, August 18, 2019, https://www.nytimes.com/in
teractive/2019/08/14/magazine/slavery-capitalism.html.

Molina, Alejandra. "'Yes in God's Backyard' to Use Church Land for
Affordable Housing." Religion News Service, November 12, 2019.
https://religionnews.com/2019/11/12/yes-in-gods-backyard-to
-use-church-land-for-affordable-housing/.

Moore, Darnell. "Self-Reflection and Social Evolution." Interview with
Krista Tippett. *On Being*, August 8, 2019. https://onbeing.org
/programs/darnell-moore-self-reflection-and-social-evolution
/#transcript.

Mudaliar, Abhilash, and Hannah Dithrich. *Sizing the Impact Investing
Market.* N.p.: Global Impact Investing Network, 2019. https://
thegiin.org/assets/Sizing%20the%20Impact%20Investing%20
Market_webfile.pdf.

The Nathan Cummings Foundation. https://nathancummings.org/ncf
-commits-to-100-percent/.

National Catholic Reporter. *Global Sisters Report Newsletter.* January 21,
2020. https://www.globalsistersreport.org/.

Overton, Matt. *Mentorship and Marketplace: A New Direction for Youth
Ministry.* San Diego: Youth Cartel, 2019.

Palmer, Parker. *The Courage to Teach: Exploring the Inner Landscape of a
Teacher's Life.* San Francisco: Jossey-Bass, 2007.

Parker, Kim, Juliana Menasce Horowitz, and Anna Brown. "About Half
of Lower-Income Americans Report Household Job or Wage
Loss Due to COVID-19." Pew Research Center, April 21, 2020.
https://www.pewsocialtrends.org/2020/04/21/about-half-of
-lower-income-americans-report-household-job-or-wage-loss
-due-to-covid-19/.

Pew Research Center. "In U.S., Decline of Christianity Continues at
Rapid Pace." October 17, 2019. https://www.pewforum.org/2019
/10/17/in-u-s-decline-of-christianity-continues-at-rapid-pace/.

Praxis Labs. *A Rule of Life for Redemptive Entrepreneurs.* New York: Praxis,
2018. Available at rule.praxislabs.org.

Princeton Theological Seminary. "Princeton Seminary and Slavery Report." Accessed July 13, 2020. https://slavery.ptsem.edu/the -report/introduction/.

Rascoe, Ayesha. "White House Touts Help for Poor Areas—but Questions Endure over Who'll Benefit." National Public Radio, July 8, 2019. https://www.npr.org/2019/07/08/736546264/white-house -touts-help-for-poor-areas-but-questions-endure-over-wholl -benefit.

Robinson, Kerry Alys. *Imagining Abundance: Fundraising, Philanthropy, and a Spiritual Call to Service.* Collegeville, MN: Liturgical Press, 2014.

Rodin, Judith, and Margot Brandenburg. *The Power of Impact Investing: Putting Markets to Work for Profit and Global Good.* Philadelphia: Wharton Digital, 2014.

Roy, Joydeep, Melissa Maynard, and Elaine Weiss. "The Hidden Costs of the Housing Crisis." Partnership for America's Economic Success. Pew Charitable Trust, 2008. https://www.pewtrusts.org/~ /media/legacy/uploadedfiles/wwwpewtrustsorg/reports/part nership_for_americas_economic_success/paeshousingreport final1pdf.pdf.

The Russell Family Foundation. https://trff.org/impact-investments/.

Sampson, Mark. "The Promise of Social Enterprise: A Theological Exploration of Faithful Economic Practice." PhD diss., King's College London, 2019.

Shanahan, Ed. "$27 Million for Reparations over Slave Ties Pledged by Seminary." *New York Times*, October 21, 2019. https://www.ny times.com/2019/10/21/nyregion/princeton-seminary-slavery -reparations.html.

Shimron, Yonat. "A North Carolina Nonprofit Helps Churches Convert Property from Liabilities into Assets." *Faith & Leadership*, February 4, 2020. https://faithandleadership.com/north-carolina-non profit-helps-churches-convert-property-liabilities-assets.

Sikora, Joanna, M. D. R. Evans, and Jonathan Kelley. "Scholarly Culture:

How Books in Adolescence Enhance Adult Literacy, Numeracy and Technology Skills in 31 Societies." *Social Science Research* 77 (January 2019). https://www.sciencedirect.com/science/article/pii/S0049089X18300607.

Simon, Morgan. *Real Impact: The New Economics of Social Change*. New York: Nation Books, 2017.

Singh, Graham. "Updating the Social Contract around Historic Places of Faith." *Municipal World*, May 2019.

Sparks, Paul, Tim Soerens, and Dwight Friesen. *The New Parish: How Neighborhood Churches Are Transforming Mission, Discipleship, and Community*. Downers Grove, IL: InterVarsity, 2014.

Twist, Lynne. *The Soul of Money: Transforming Your Relationship with Money and Life*. New York: Norton, 2017.

Villanueva, Edgar. *Decolonizing Wealth*. Oakland, CA: Berrett-Koehler Publishers, 2018.

"Why VCs Aren't Funding Women-led Startups." Wharton School of Business, May 24, 2016. https://knowledge.wharton.upenn.edu/article/vcs-arent-funding-women-led-startups/.

Women's Philanthropy Institute. *How Women and Men Approach Impact Investing*. Lilly Family School of Philanthropy, 2018. https://scholarworks.iupui.edu/bitstream/handle/1805/16229/Impact%20Investing%20Report%20FINAL.pdf.

Working Capital for Community Needs. *20 Years of Socially Responsible Investing in Their Own Words*. Madison, WI: Working Capital for Community Needs, 2011.

World Health Organization. *Tobacco and Its Environmental Impact: An Overview*. Geneva: World Health Organization, 2017. https://apps.who.int/iris/bitstream/handle/10665/255574/9789241512497-eng.pdf.

# Index

# Index

# Index